MAINLY KENT

CHRISTOPHER WRIGHT
with sketches by Helen Wright

Dedication
MAZ
with love and
gratitude

Published by Christopher Wright
Pond Cottages
Adisham
Canterbury
Kent CT3 3JJ

Tel: 01304 840106

First published October 1997
ISBN 0 9531997 0 3

Printed by
Mickle Print Ltd
Westminster Road, Canterbury, Kent

Tel: 01227 780001

Contents

Acknowledgements

Mr Harry Margary of Lympne Castle

Mr Terry Williams, Director of the Maritime Museum, Deal

The Dover Museum for the reproduction of Turner's *Deal*

The Arms and Armour Press for permission to reproduce the photograph
' Manning the Mast' in Kenneth Poolman's *British Sailor* (1989)

Ms Ann Chumbley of the Turner Study Room at the Tate Gallery

The Headmistress of Gad's Hill School, Rochester

Mr Martin Child for his song *On the Map*

Mrs Valerie House for her help with *Over and Under the Earth*.

Illustrations

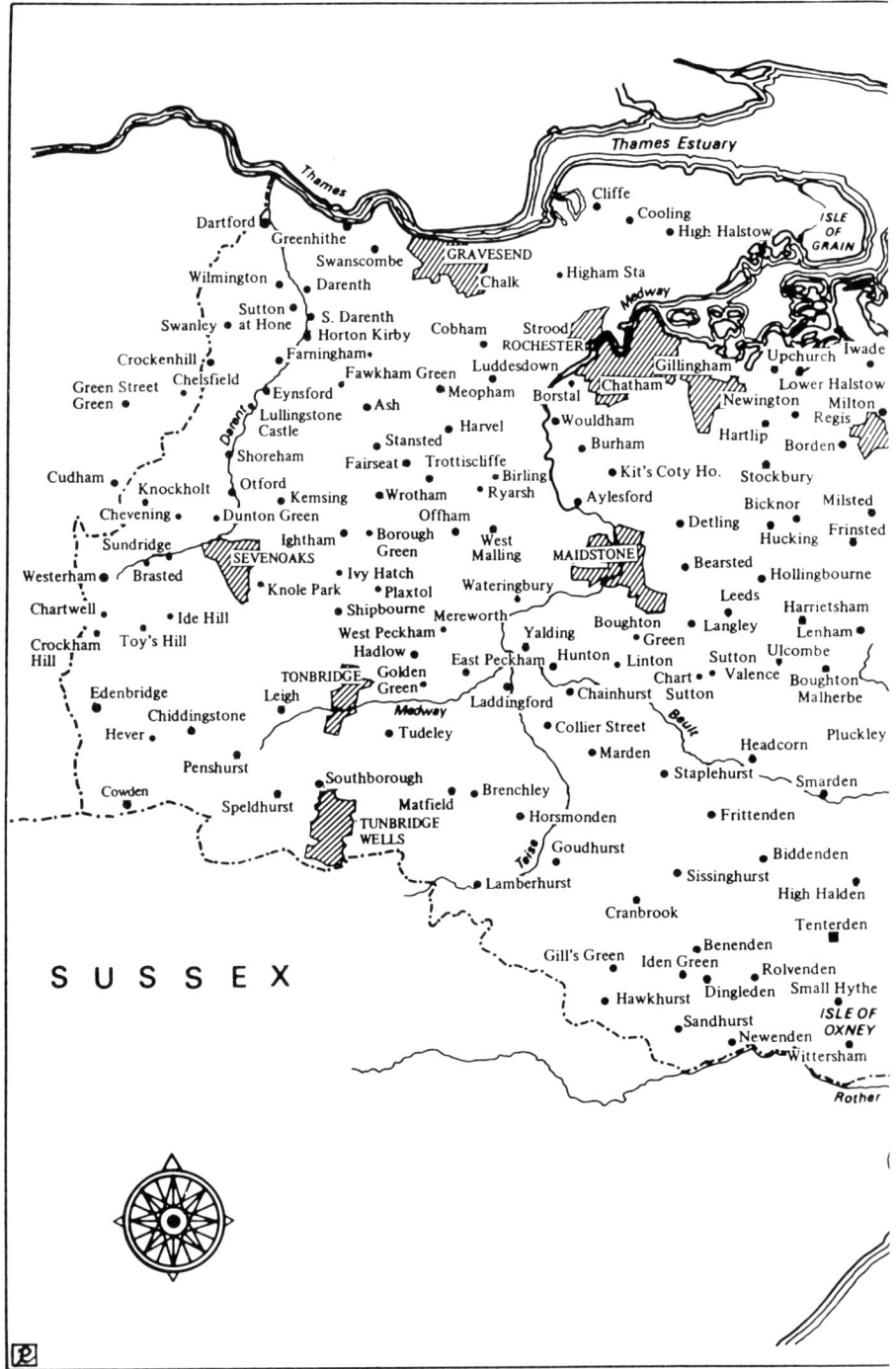

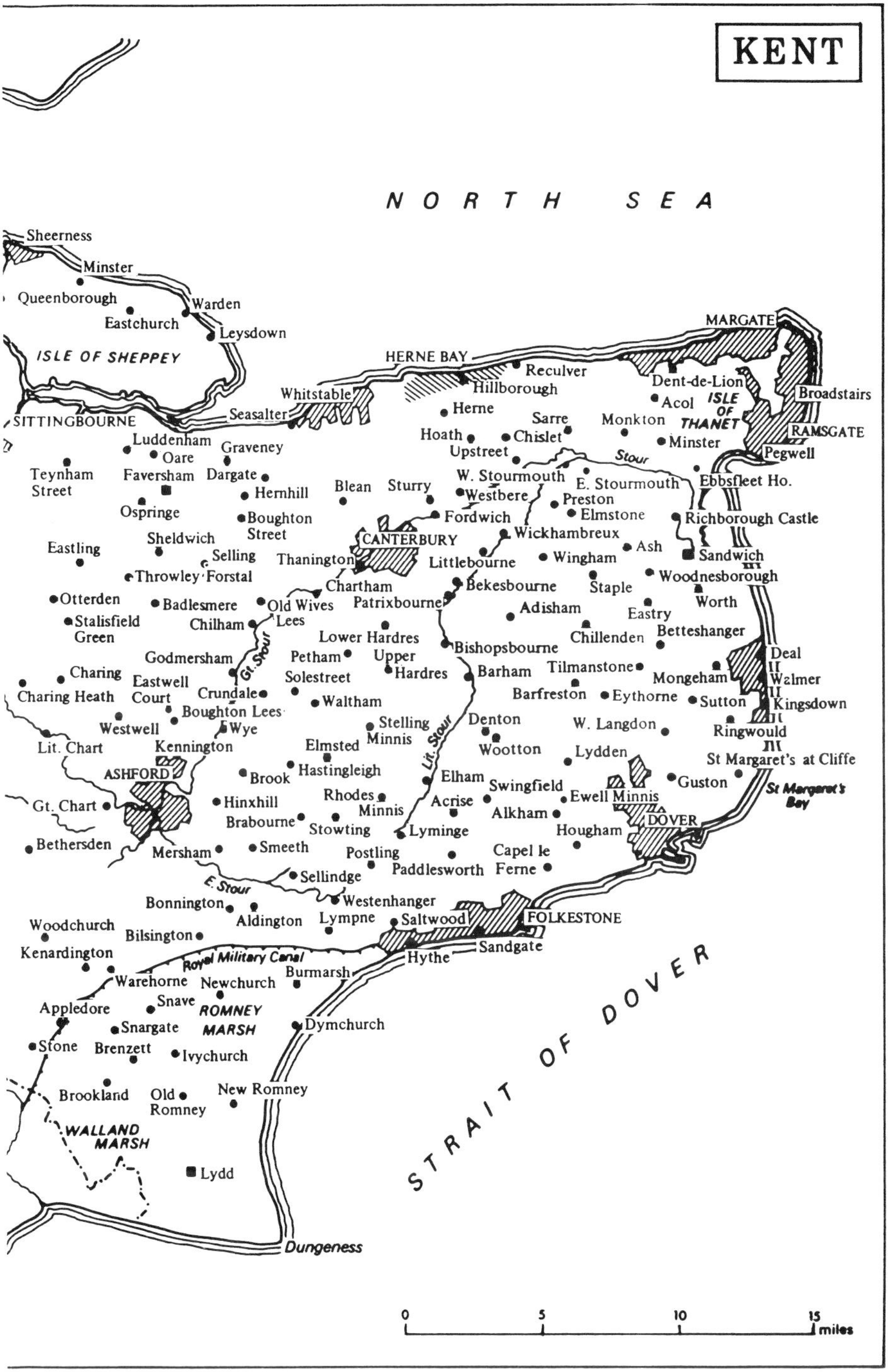
KENT
NORTH SEA
Sheerness
Minster
Queenborough
Warden
Eastchurch
Leysdown
ISLE OF SHEPPEY
SITTINGBOURNE
Seasalter
Whitstable
HERNE BAY
Hillborough
Reculver
MARGATE
Dent-de-Lion
Acol
ISLE OF THANET
Broadstairs
RAMSGATE
Pegwell
Minster
Monkton
Sarre
Herne
Hoath
Chislet
Upstreet
Stour
Luddenham
Oare
Graveney
Teynham Street
Faversham
Dargate
Hernhill
Blean
Sturry
W. Stourmouth
E. Stourmouth
Westbere
Preston
Ebbsfleet Ho.
Ospringe
Boughton Street
Fordwich
Elmstone
Richborough Castle
Sheldwich
CANTERBURY
Wickhambreux
Eastling
Selling
Thanington
Littlebourne
Wingham
Ash
Sandwich
Throwley Forstal
Chartham
Staple
Woodnesborough
Otterden
Badlesmere
Old Wives Lees
Patrixbourne
Bekesbourne
Adisham
Eastry
Worth
Stalisfield Green
Chilham
Lower Hardres
Chillenden
Betteshanger
Godmersham
Petham
Upper Hardres
Bishopsbourne
Deal
Gt. Stour
Charing
Eastwell Court
Solestreet
Barham
Tilmanstone
Mongeham
Walmer
Charing Heath
Crundale
Waltham
Barfreston
Eythorne
Sutton
Kingsdown
Westwell
Boughton Lees
Stelling Minnis
Denton
W. Langdon
Ringwould
Lit. Chart
Wye
Kennington
Elmsted
Wootton
Lydden
St Margaret's at Cliffe
Lit. Stour
ASHFORD
Brook
Hastingleigh
Elham
Swingfield
Guston
St Margaret's Bay
Gt. Chart
Hinxhill
Rhodes Minnis
Acrise
Ewell Minnis
Brabourne
Stowting
Alkham
DOVER
Bethersden
Lyminge
Hougham
Mersham
Smeeth
Postling
Capel le Ferne
Paddlesworth
Sellindge
E. Stour
Westenhanger
Bonnington
Aldington
Woodchurch
Lympne
Saltwood
FOLKESTONE
Bilsington
Sandgate
Kenardington
Royal Military Canal
Hythe
Warehorne
Newchurch
Burmarsh
Appledore
Snave
ROMNEY MARSH
Snargate
Dymchurch
Stone
Brenzett
Ivychurch
STRAIT OF DOVER
Brookland
Old Romney
New Romney
WALLAND MARSH
Lydd
Dungeness
0
5
10
15 miles

1

THE LANDSCAPE OF
GREAT EXPECTATIONS
The Five Little Lozenges
and the Terrible Hulks

GREAT EXPECTATIONS is one of my favourite novels. I loved it long before I came to live in Kent and when I did so I found that a knowledge of the Hundred of Hoo, 'the marsh country, down by the river,*' as Dickens called it, made me love it more. So I took to exploring the area, and went first to Cooling, about twenty years ago, on a cold April day.

Cooling stands close to the Gravesend reach of the Thames. In the graveyard of its church lie the tombstones which are generally thought to be the originals of 'the five little stone lozenges . . . sacred to the memory of five little brothers of mine' with which the novel opens. So I decided to emulate Dickens and to start where he started - at Cooling.

The guidebook suggested that I go first to Lodge Hill, the highest point for many miles around, and gain a good view of both the Thames and the Medway estuaries. Dark black clouds and stinging showers foraged inland from the Thames. Their assaults seemed like those of the French pirates whose raids, six hundred years ago, led Sir John de Cobham to build Cooling Castle to defend his surrounding estates. As I set off I remembered Dickens' description of the scene now before me, as seen through the eyes of the six-year old Pip:-

'My first most vivid and broad impression of the identity of things seems to me to have been gained on a memorable raw afternoon towards evening. At such a time I found out for certain . . . that the

* The Medway

dark flat wilderness beyond the churchyard, intersected with dykes and mounds and gates, with scattered cattle feeding on it, was the marshes; and that the low leaden line beyond was the river; and that the distant savage lair, from which the wind was rushing, was the sea; and that the small bundle of shivers growing afraid of it all and beginning to cry was Pip.'

I felt very much like Pip as I walked over the hedgeless landscape, past fields of cabbages with a few rectangular workers blowing on their fingers, under the double row of striding pylons, to come face to face with an enormous hostile dog which ran onto the road from a nearby riding school and barred my path. He let me pass, however, merely sniffing my turn ups from behind as I walked by his gate, while five gaunt horses, excited by the high winds, charged round the perimeter of their field, whinnying. It was difficult not to break into a run once the danger appeared over but I hope I seemed unconcerned as I turned into a bridle path and made for Lodge Hill. The menace of the marshes, however, which was to stay with me all day, was not to be shaken off so easily.

I found myself in a waste land of old gun emplacements, nissen huts, 'Danger - Army Exercises in Progress' signs, dumped lorries, motor bicycles, cars, even an entire aeroplane in process of rusting away. Above, a helicopter circled the vast dump - for this is what the Hill has become - while a man studied me from behind the curtains of a farmhouse window, his yard littered with the shells of racing and stock cars. Soon he came out, flanked by a retinue of barking dogs, and suggested, courteously enough, that I retrace my footsteps since I could go no further. There seemed little alternative, so I settled for an early pub lunch.

The sun now appeared with traditional April flirtatiousness and shone brilliantly on the round white oil tanks of Thames Haven, on the Essex side of the estuary. In the foreground the marsh landmarks appeared, curiously merged in the haze. Though separated in time of building by hundreds of years, and serving sharply different functions, the squat towers of the churches at High Halstow, Cliffe and Cooling, the towers of the oil refineries and power stations on both banks of the river, and the round towers of Cooling Castle all seemed part of the marsh scene. Even a tanker moving downstream to the mouth of the estuary appeared like one of the hulks from which Pip's terrifying convict had escaped - until you realised it was moving.

The pub at Cooling where I sought refuge displays rules of the house, dated 1786, which suit its forbidding environs:-

'No thieves, fakirs, rogues or tinkers.
No skulking loafers or flea-bitten tramps.
No slap or tickle of the wenches.
No banging of tankards on the tables.
No cockfighting.
Flintlocks, cudgels, daggers and swords to be handed
to the innkeeper for safe-keeping.'

On top of these prohibitions, they had no sandwiches, so I drove into Cliffe for a beefburger, a walk round the village's vast low-bodied church, and a view over the marshes which at that point soon join the mud flats of the estuary.

The wind was rising steadily, the whine of the telegraph wires was growing shriller and shriller, and I couldn't muster the necessary endurance for a tour of the ruins of Cooling Castle, whose moat is still filled, and whose gatehouse stands unimpaired, a landmark for miles around. But I walked round the outer defences, and saw the bodies of four rats swaying in the wind from the branch of a tree, a grim reminder of the creaking iron chains in which the bodies of criminals would have been hanged in Pip's time.

So I turned at last to the graveyard of Cooling Church, and there, just outside the south door, by the path, were the tombstones:-

'As I never saw my father or my mother, and never saw any likeness of either of them (for their days were long before the days of photographs) my first fancies of what they were like were unreasonably derived from their tombstones. The shape of the letters on my father's, gave me an odd idea that he was a square, stout, dark man, with curly black hair. From the character and turn of the

inscription 'Also Georgiana Wife of the Above' I drew a childish conclusion that my mother was freckled and sickly. To five little stone lozenges, each about a foot and a half long, which were arranged in a neat row beside their grave, and were sacred to the memory of five little brothers of mine - who gave up trying to get a living exceedingly early in that universal struggle - I am indebted for a belief I religiously entertained that they had all been born on their backs with their hands in their trouser-pockets, and had never taken them out in this existence.'

Cooling Churchyard

There are in fact thirteen little lozenges not five and their sizes are adapted to the respective ages of the infants. Much of the writing on the stones is nearly indecipherable but I made out the date of May 1770 followed by eight months, six days; then William, who died in June 1773, seven months and two weeks; another aged eleven months, one week, and six days; and another aged four months and six days.

The children were members of the Comport family, who lived in the farmhouse, built within the walls of the castle towards the end of the eighteenth century. Seven of them came from the farming family; all of them died before they were two. Those children whom Mrs Comport managed to rear to adult life were as unlucky as their parents. The other infants, whose remains lie under the stone lozenges were all Comport offspring. The name of the last of them can just be read on the stone:- 'John Rose Baker, died June 9, 1837, aged one month'. Dickens began work on *Great Expectations* twenty three years after his death.

As I was noting the inscriptions I was expecting a terrible voice to cry 'Hold your noise' and a man to 'start up from among the graves' at the side of the church porch, shouting 'Keep still, you little devil, or I'll cut your throat'.

There is something about a peninsular that comes to a point which always leads me on restless and frustrated, until I reach the final tip of land, and the open sea before it. The map seemed to suggest that at All-Hallows-on-Sea I could see the open estuary, and that the end of Kent, between the Medway and the Thames, was a vast waste of power stations and oil refineries on the Isle of Grain, tenuously separated from the mainland by Yantlet Creek - and so it proved. I sat amongst the deserted All Hallows holiday chalets, and amusement centres, the empty ice cream kiosks and kiddies' playgrounds, with a wind howling about my ears like the sound track of a horror film, and looked across the Thames to Essex.

The world was all sky and scudding cloud and wheeling birds. A red funnelled ship made its way through freshly painted buoys up the choppy river and the sun suddenly picked out a clump of trees on the

Essex hills that look down on the industrial wasteland of the water front. But this was not the end of the peninsular and it was no good pretending it was. The end was the northern tip of the Isle of Grain - Grain Point.

The Isle of Grain to which I now drove might prove one great no-go area, but I decided I had to go there. Certainly it must have more 'No Unauthorised Entry' signs than any part of England not owned by the Ministry of Defence. But no one could prevent harmless exploration. So I drove on and on through a vast churned-up moonscape of storage tanks and towers, of cranes, and derricks, of low buildings and high voltage cables humming in the eternal marsh wind. Nobody challenged me and I left the car by a minor moon crater, to walk the last few hundred yards.

Suddenly out of the devitalised dusty grass embankment on the skyline rose an enormous tanker, its body as long as the nave of Canterbury Cathedral, flying the Stars and Stripes, and moored alongside Grain Point. High net fences finally barred my way and I could go no further. Here was the twentieth century's addition to the gaunt and frightening world of the marshes. The hulks, where Pip's convicts had lived and French prisoners of war before them, confined like animals in a cruel zoo, had gone. In their place had come this alien though beautiful world of oil and gas storage tanks, of industrial chimneys and towers, of tankers sailing up the river as if, so flat are the surrounding marshes, they are sailing on land, and of huge ships moored off the Kentish coast.

A storm was driving towards us from Sheppey. The black horizon was striped and dappled with the white smoke of the power stations. It was time to go. As I drove away past five silly frightened sheep, which had somehow strayed into this vision of the end of the world, I thought once more of *Great Expectations*. I remembered the account of the captured convict's return to the hulks from which he had escaped, and of how Pip had watched him go. The words became symbols of the light and the dark. There on the marshes in the high winds and the terrifying hulks lay the alien dark which surrounds the cosy, companionable light of blacksmith's Joe Gargery's forge. And

Pip stood there in the darkness, peeping out from behind Joe's comforting presence, watching it all, as the convict is rowed back to prison:-

'No one seemed surprised to see him, or interested in seeing him, or glad to see him, or sorry to see him, or spoke a word, except that somebody in the boat growled as if to dogs, 'Give way, you', which was the signal for the dip of the oars. By the light of the torches, we saw the black Hulk lying out a little way from the mud of the shore, like a wicked Noah's ark. Cribbed and barred and moored by massive rusty chains, the prison-ship seemed in my young eyes to be ironed like the prisoners. We saw the boat go alongside, and we saw him taken up the side and disappear. Then, the ends of the torches were flung hissing into the water, and went out, as if it were all over with him.'

2

AROUND GAD'S HILL

SOME TIME had passed since my visit to Cooling and Grain Point, and I had been diverted to other things. But I never forgot the marshes and returned to them - again it was April - one Saturday afternoon when the traffic along the main Gravesend - Rochester road was even more continuous than usual. I had parked my car near Gad's Hill Place, where Dickens wrote *Great Expectations*, and when I wanted to drive across the road to join the lane opposite, loyally named Forge Lane, the wait seemed interminable. As I waited I thought of Dickens setting out after lunch on one of his afternoon walks. (They averaged 12 miles a day, and took two and a half hours). I had just finished my sandwiches, and reckoned that if Dickens would have enjoyed a more formal lunch (though it was always a light one) we would have been setting off at much the same time. I, however, did not intend to gesticulate wildly, or mouth sentences, as I walked. Dickens, no doubt rehearsing tomorrow's chapter, used to alarm those who passed him on the road by doing just that.

Dickens was always interested in his appearance - his neckties, his velvet jackets and waistcoats, his gold watch chain, the red geranium in his button hole (white for his public readings, like the waist coat). By the time he moved to Gad's Hill he had a long moustache, curled at the ends, and a straight beard which reached to the tie-knot. He had no side whiskers and no hair on his cheeks so that most of his face was clear of hair. But though he was always the dandy, he naturally dressed more casually for his walks. The landlady of the 'Crispin and Christianus', an inn just outside Strood, where he liked to call during his walks, remembered him as wearing:

'low shoes not over-well mended, loose large check-patterned trousers that sometimes got entangled in the shoes when walking, a brown coat thrown open, sometimes without waistcoat, a belt instead of braces, a necktie which now and then got round towards his ear, and a large felt hat, similar to an American's, set well at the back of his head.'

He would ask for a glass of ale or a little cold brandy-and-water. Then, 'He sat down at the corner of the settle ... He rarely spoke to anyone but looked around as though taking in everything at a glance ...' (Ackroyd op.cit. pages 926-7)

He was, of course, something of a local spectacle as he walked with head held high and at a great pace. Some would follow him, or try to get a better and second view of him, by turning round a corner and returning the opposite way from that in which they had originally been walking. He walked in the middle of the road, and said 'good day' or nodded to passers by, without engaging them in conversation, unless they were children.

He was a man of regular habits, writing - come hell or high water - every morning and walking every afternoon. (The evenings were given over to sociability.) When, earlier in his life, he had been writing *David Copperfield* in his little study at Fort House, Broadstairs, overlooking the Channel, he claimed that he always stopped at one o'clock prompt, after his four hour morning stint. At the first stroke of the lunch gong he would down pens, even in the middle of a sentence, rather than run one second over time. For, contrary to general belief, he hated writing and was delighted when the time was up.

I was making for Lower Higham but took a wrong turning and found myself on the edge of Gravesend. The cosy suburban road, where finally I stopped, was called, most inappropriately, 'Orlick Road'. It made me think I hadn't strayed too far from my way. Sure enough I was soon driving back into Lower Higham.

Dickens was far too imaginative an artist to be tied to exact locations. He had suffered in the past from people who had accused him of holding them up to ridicule in his novels, or of maligning their villages. So no single village can be called Pip's. It is a combination of several. Lower Higham is one of these, as is Cooling and Hoo St. Werburgh, and seems to have had strong qualifications. There was a windmill, whose base still exists, a wheelwright's shop, a saw pit, and the all-important forge - though all now have gone. The turnpike road that ran between Strood and Chalk, which Pip walked, ran through Lower Higham. But if 'The Jolly Bargeman', where Joe liked to smoke his pipe of an evening, was in the village it has been knocked down. This left the church, described as being a mile from the village. Nobody in the tall, ugly modern pub seemed to know of its whereabouts, so I assumed that if I drove along Church Road I would come to it. This proved to be the case.

On the outskirts of the village absorbed men lay underneath their cars by the side of the road and I had to drive slowly to avoid them. Their gardens shone in the sun with frothy pink artificial cherry blossom, but I doubt if their owners had time to spare them a glance. Finally a mile from the village I parked my car outside St. Mary's, Higham, being careful to avoid another car maintenance man nearby. His feet alone were visible. He kicked them wildly to give himself more power as he struggled to undo a nut.

In the churchyard I found, at last, a friendly and talkative marshman - or rather woman. A large red-faced lady was creaking over a grave, on which she was planting some bulbs. She stood up finally, gasping as she raised herself, and explained that her arthritis came from her early years, when she followed the horses as they ploughed the fields round about. She remembered watching the crew filming the post-war *Great Expectations* on the marshes nearby - the one with John Mills and Alec Guiness. When she had stumped off to her husband, who was in need of his tea, I went into the churchyard.

There were six lozenge-shaped tombstones to the right of the main church door, near a magnificent yew tree but it seems likely that Dickens transplanted his 'lozenges' from Cooling Churchyard to St.

Mary's, Higham. The latter is not only the right distance from the village. It has a steeple like Pip's village church, whereas Cooling Church has not. Above all it is surrounded by marshes.

Like Pip, I sat on a seat out of the wind and looked over the 'dark, flat winderness' still 'intersected with dykes and mounds and gates'. I sat there, expecting to hear again the convict's terrible voice. In my mind's eye I could see that 'fearful man, all in coarse grey, with a great iron on his leg. A man with no hat, and with broken shoes, and with an old rag tied round his head. A man who had been soaked in water, and smothered in mud, and lamed by stones, and cut by flints, and stung by nettles, and torn by briars'. I could see him as he 'limped, and shivered, and glared and growled and whose teeth chattered in his head as he seized me by the chin'.

I gazed out over the marshes towards Cliffe. The Thames still formed 'a low, leaden line' on the horizon. Nothing much had changed in the Thames direction, though the eastern view towards the Medway was now dominated by Kingsnorth Power Station and the multitude of bungalows surrounding it. The marshes were as bleak as ever, its people as self-contained.

I had been reading W L Gadd's *Great Expectations' Country* which reconstructs the marshland scenes with meticulous detail. I could see it all. There to the west of Cliffe the gibbet would have stood, and there 'the beacon by which the sailors steered - like an unhooped cask upon a pole' - the 'only two black things in all the prospect that seemed to be standing up right.' Nearby was the 'old battery' where Pip had tried unavailingly to teach Joe his ABC. And near again was the 'sluice-house' where Pip so nearly met his death at the hands of Orlick.

Once again Dicken's jig-saw methods of topography had been at work. The beacon in Dicken's time did indeed stand at the mouth of Cliffe Creek. There had been a beacon there since the fourteenth century, when Richard II had placed one as an alarm in case the French sailed up the Thames. More recently it was used as a navigating mark for ships sailing up river. But the nearest gibbet on the Thames, when Dickens was writing *Great Expectations*, stood

19

between Northfleet and Gravesend. Dickens was probably drawing on his memories of the gibbet which stood on the Medway marshes above Upnor Castle. He would have seen it from the dockyard on the other side of the river when, as a boy, he had visited the dockyard with his father.

The 'old battery' was demolished a few years after the publication of *Great Expectations* when Cliffe Fort was built on the same spot. It had stood by the edge of the Thames for many years. Henry VIII had anticipated French invasion - this time in the sixteenth century - and had built the gun battery as part of a chain of defences which ran along the south coast to Portsmouth.

The 'hulks' from which Magwitch had escaped were also transplanted by Dickens' imagination. He seems to have placed them in Egypt Bay, five miles from the churchyard and four from the battery, where the soldiers had captured Magwitch and his enemy that Christmas evening. There was a 'hulk' at Egypt Bay, but it was a coastguard ship and not a prison ship. Dickens probably transferred the prison ships which stood by Upnor Castle, which he knew, to Egypt Bay, for the purposes of his novel. From the old battery the party took 'a reasonably good path', after floundering and flopping in the 'death-cold flats'. The convicts were lame and it took the party 'an hour or so' to reach the landing place, from which the convicts were rowed back to their hulk. This would be the right amount of time to take along the sea wall from Cliffe Fort to Egypt Bay, and at this point Dickens is describing exactly the lie of the land as it existed around 1860. He had probably walked the four miles himself.

As for the sluice-house, where Pip so nearly met his death at Orlick's hands, it stood close to the head of Cliffe Creek. It stood beside the sluice-gates connecting the Creek with the canal to the chalk quarry, where the lime kilns in the novel were situated. Pip would have walked, in answer to the mysterious anonymous letter he had received in his London lodgings, the five miles and more from Rochester through Strood to Cliffe. He would then have floundered along a muddy, slippery, flinty path to the sluice house for the best part of an hour. He would have done this on a dark night in a 'melancholy wind'.

Pip comments that 'the marshes were so very dismal a stranger would have found them insupportable, and even to me they were so oppressive that I hesitated, half inclined to go back'. Indeed at this point, Dickens strains our credulity. Here is Pip, one arm in a sling and painful to the touch. (He had recently tried to save the burning Miss Havisham's life when her ancient wedding dress had caught fire.) He was walking for two hours and more in answer to an anonymous letter which called him to an unexplained meeting, miles from human habitation at 9 o'clock on a dark night. It is difficult not to think that Dickens was putting Pip through dangers he would not in fact have run for the sake of creating a dramatic scene.

Once again of course, Dickens has altered the topography. He makes the lime-kiln closer to the sluice gate than was the case in real life. There is no stone quarry on the marshes. The sluice-house must have been in good enough condition in Dicken's time if it was still standing in 1929 when Mr Gadd reported it as being in good state. The sluice was certainly not abandoned, as Dickens describes it. Once again we have to shake ourselves and remind ourselves that Dickens is not writing a guide book but a novel.

After such a mental journey it was quite a struggle not to try the walk across the marshes to Cliffe and Egypt Bay. But I decided to stick to my plans and visit Hoo St. Werburgh. I wanted to see another possible contender for the honour of being Pip's village.

Hoo St. Werburgh's Churchyard, for all its surrounding suburban development and the dominance of nearby Kingsnorth Power Station, seemed as bleak as the rest of marshland. Here too, as in so many Kentish churchyards, were lozenge-shaped tombstones with well established headstones nearby. I sat in the sun, which was as cold as ever, while the wind punched the church with deadly jabs, and looked out again at the marshes. I thought how glad I was that it was 1996 and daylight. At least Magwitch was not suddenly going to erupt on me. At least we had given up using prison-ships, though the present Home Secretary might soon turn back to them in despair having tried everything else. At least, unlike those lying under the lozenges or headstones, I did not risk catching typhus, cholera, or malaria from the marsh mosquitoes.

It was time to cheer myself up so I drove to Frindsbury. Dickens didn't like only to tramp the marshes, sit in marsh churchyards, and peer at marsh forges and pubs. He loved most of all to sit by the open water of the Medway, as it begins to widen out on its way to where it joins the Thames Estuary, and, as he put it, to 'idle'.

I had been reading his description in *The Uncommercial Traveller* (p.260 Oxford Edition) and had been caught up in the exuberant details of his vision:-

'There are some small out-of-the-way landing-places on the Thames and the Medway, where I do much of my summer idling. Running water is favourable to day-dreams, and a strong tidal river is the best of running water for mine. I like to watch the great ships standing out to sea or coming home richly laden, the active little steam-tugs confidently puffing with them to and from the sea-horizon, the fleet of barges that seem to have plucked their brown and russet sails from the ripe trees in the landscape, the heavy old colliers, light in ballast, floundering down before the tide; the light screw barks and schooners imperiously holding a straight course while the others patiently tack and go about, the yachts with their tiny hulls and great white sheets of canvas, the little sailing-boats bobbing to and fro on their errands of pleasure or business, and - as it is the nature of little people to do - making a prodigious fuss about their small affairs.'

So I sat in the car park of the 'Ship Inn' at Frindsbury - one of Dicken's favourite 'out of the way landing places', though you would never think so now, with its drinkers packed as closely together outside the pub as the little moored yachts off the jetty - and looked out across the river to the distant red brick line of Chatham Dockyard.

The cold sun shone, the mast wires of the anchored yachts tinkled without ceasing, the yachts out in the estuary nearly keeled over in the wind. The world of the estuary was a world away in spirit, if only a few hundred yards in space, from the dark and threatening world of the marshes.

And more and more I began to doubt the truth of Dicken's words. 'Idling'? Dickens was one of the most hard-working men who ever lived. He had even, with Macbeth, 'conquered sleep'. He would tramp the streets of London during much of the night and emerge, after three hours' sleep, at 9am in his study, fresh of phrase and sharp of mind, to begin the morning spell of writing. And it was then, when the tap of the unconscious was turned full on and the sentences flowed, that the results of the 'Idling' appeared on the page.

The climax of *Great Expectations* is the description of Pip's abortive attempt to smuggle Abel Magwitch out of England by persuading a steamer, travelling from London down the Thames Estuary, to take him on board:

'Our plan was this. The tide, beginning to run down at nine, and being with us until three, we intended still to creep on after it had turned, and row against it until dark. We should then be well in those long reaches below Gravesend, between Kent and Essex, where the river is broad and solitary, where the water-side inhabitants are very few, and where lone public-houses are scattered here and there, of which we could choose one for a resting-place. There we meant to lie by, all night.' (Chapter 54)

So Pip and Herbert Pocket set out stealthily in a rowing boat to pick Magwitch up:

'Again among the tiers of shipping, in and out, avoiding rusty chain-cables, frayed hempen hawsers and bobbing buoys, sinking for the moment floating broken baskets, scattering floating chips of wood and shaving, cleaving floating scum of coal, in and out under the figure-head of the "John" of Sunderland . . . and the "Betsy" of Yarmouth with a firm formality of bosom and her knobby eyes starting two inches out of her head, in and out, hammers going in ship-builders' yards, saws going at timber, clashing engines going at things unknown, pumps going in leaky ships, capstans going, ships going out to sea, and unintelligible sea-creatures roaring curses over the bulwarks at respondent lightermen, in and out - out at last upon the clearer river . . .' (Chapter 54)

Great Expectations was begun in 1860. By this time Dickens was living in Gad's Hill Place, having left London two years earlier. His marriage had broken down, and much of his increasingly wild energy was spent on his public readings and on the pounding itinerary which he had concocted so that he could reach the largest amount of people in the shortest amount of time. When he was writing 'Great Expectations' he was rarely going to London, and would have had little time to 'idle' by the upper reaches of the Thames. He would most probably have been sitting where I was sitting - at Frindsbury and Upnor. And he would have been listening to the noises of "The Achilles" construction at Chatham Dockyard, an iron-plated ship, the noises of whose building rang across the Medway:

'Ding, Clash, Dong, BANG, Boom, Rattle, Clash, BANG, Clink, BANG, Dong, BANG, Clatter, BANG BANG BANG! What on earth is this! This is, or soon will be, the "Achilles", iron armour-plated ship. Twelve hundred men are working at her now; twelve hundred men working on stages over her sides, over her bows, over her stern, under her keel, between her decks, down in her hold, within her and without, crawling and creeping into the finest curves of her lines wherever it is possible for men to twist. Twelve hundred hammerers, measurers, caulkers, armourers, forgers, smiths, shipwrights; twelve hundred dingers, clashers, dongers, rattlers, clinkers, bangers bangers bangers!'

The Uncommercial Traveller p.263 (Oxford)

Or he might have been visiting the yard itself to get a closer view of proceedings, as he loved to do.

When he looked across the Medway, and eastwards to where that river joins the Thames at the Nore, he would have been doing so at just about the most busy time in either river's long history. By mid-century sail was given way to paddle-steam and straight steam. The days of the great sailing clippers were coming to an end. Pip and Herbert Pocket were trying to smuggle Magwitch on board a paddle-steamer bound for Hamburg. The russet-sailed barges, the yachts, and little sailing boats jostled for position, as in Dickens' description earlier, with steam-tugs, light screw barks and steamers. And these, as Dickens describes them, have all the confidence of those who revel in their use of the latest invention and look down upon the lesser creatures of sail. They 'imperiously hold a straight course' or go 'confidently puffing' to the horizon. The scene spread out before Dickens as he sat on the northern banks of the Medway shouted at him with its exhilaration, and bustle, its teeming, pulsing life, and inexhaustible variety.

No - whatever he might say, even if he actually believed it, this workaholic was not 'idling'. Or rather the 'idling' did its work. When he returned to his desk the next morning Dickens, a notoriously quick writer, drew on his experiences of earlier times, sitting quietly by the river. The Medway from Chatham to Grain Point became the Thames as it stretches from Gravesend to the river's mouth. Not a minute of 'idling' time was wasted. It had watered the seeds of his imagination. The flowers grew on the pages of his novel to full and wonderful bloom.

3

LIFE at GAD'S HILL PLACE

FOR A MAN to whom the boundaries between fact and fantasy were always blurred, Dickens' purchase of Gad's Hill Place marked the supreme example of a dream come true. The feelings of personal triumph which accompanied his final acquisition of the Place shine through his account of his encounter with 'a very queer small boy', written some time during his negotiations with its owner.

In his *Uncommercial Traveller* Dickens describes a journey he took by coach from London along the Old Kent Road to Dover.

'So smooth was the old high road, and so fresh were the horses, and so fast went I that it was midway between Gravesend and Rochester, and the widening river was bearing the ships, white-sailed or black smoked, out to sea, when I noticed by the wayside a very queer small boy.

'Holloa' said I, to the very queer small boy, 'where do you live?'

'At Chatham', says he . . .

I took him up in a moment, and we went on. Presently, the very queer small boy says, 'This is Gad's-hill we are coming to, where Falstaff went out to rob those travellers, and ran away.'

'You know something about Falstaff, eh?' said I.

'All about him' said the very queer small boy. 'I am old (I am nine) and I read all sorts of books. But do let us stop at the top of the hill, and look at the house there, if you please!'

'You admire that house?' said I.

'Bless you, sir,' said the very queer small boy 'when I was not more than half as old as nine, it used to be a treat for me to be brought to look at it. And ever since I can recollect, my father, seeing me so fond of it, has often said to me, "If you were to be very persevering and were to work hard, you might some day come to live in it." Though that's impossible!' said the very queer small boy . . .' I was rather amazed to be told this by the very queer small boy; for that house happens to be my house and I have reason to believe that what he said was true.' ('Travelling Abroad', No.7 in *The Uncommercial Traveller* Oxford.)

Dickens had coveted the house on the top of Gad's Hill - half way between Gravesend and Rochester - ever since early childhood. The Hill is five miles - five very steep and dusty miles - from Number Two Ordnance Terrace, Chatham, where the Dickens family lived from the year when Charles was five to that in which he was ten. John Dickens walked there with his son on several Sunday afternoons. En route he took the opportunity, in true nineteenth century style, of pointing out to Charles the prizes which can fall into the laps of the persistently ambitious.

On 7 February, 1855 - Dickens' 43rd birthday - Dickens was in Gravesend. It was a very cold day, and the roads were thick with snow. Nevertheless Dickens was determined to walk the thirteen miles to Rochester, one of his favourite walks, and when he saw that the Dover Road was cleared, with walls of snow up to six feet high on either side, he set off with his usual determination. To his joy and amazement he saw a 'For Sale' notice outside Gad's Hill Place.

From now on, Dickens acted in a hot flush of decisiveness. The recent owner had only died a few days earlier, on 1st February, though the tenant, the local vicar, was still living there. On February 9 Dickens wrote to a friend and fellow-journalist W H Wills:-

'When I was at Gravesend t'other day, I saw at Gad's Hill - just opposite . . . where your charmer Miss Lynn used to live - a little freehold to be sold. The spot and the very house are literally 'a dream of my childhood' and I should like to look at it before I go to Paris. With that purpose I must go to Strood by the North Kent, at a quarter-past ten tomorrow morning, and I want you, strongly booted, to go with me. (I know the particulars from the agent.)' (Quoted Alan Watts - *Dickens at Gad's Hill*, Chapter 2.)

By extraordinary chance the new owner, Mrs Lynn Linton, a contributor to Dickens' *Household Words*, was dining shortly afterwards, in a house where Wills was a fellow diner. Wills was asked to take Mrs. Linton down to dinner. It soon came out that she knew the Higham area well:

'I was a child there', she told Wills, who immediately passed on the news to Dickens 'in the house they call Gad's Hill Place. My father was the rector and lived there many years. He has just died, and left it to me, and I want to sell it.'

Wills dashed to see Dickens the very next morning. 'It is written' he said 'that you were to have that house at Gad's Hill. So you must buy it. Now or never.'

Later, Dickens just commented succinctly:

'I did.'

Dickens had a strong feeling that certain developments particularly if they happened on his birthday, were 'meant'. Of all these, his occupation of Gad's Hill Place was one of the closest to his heart. Nevertheless at first he professed himself very cool about the house. He was at pains to point out that it was to be only a 'summer house' and for only three months of the summer at that. His 'proper' residence was still Tavistock House in London. It was his final separation from his wife, Catherine, which led to his last and permanent move.

In April 1858, after years of increasingly public quarrelling, Dickens finally stormed out of Tavistock House. Catherine's parents had come to stay, provoking Dickens to a final outburst that he could not 'bear the contemplation of their imbecility any more.' He walked the thirty miles from Tavistock House to Gad's Hill Place through the night, arriving there in the morning. From now on, until his death twelve years later, Gad's Hill was to be his home. His sister-in-law Catherine Hogarth kept his house, together with his eldest daughter Mamie. His other eight children came and went, as did Dickens himself, as he travelled all over the country and North America on his exhausting public reading tours. But it was always to Gad's Hill that he returned.

Great Expectations was finally completed in the summer of 1861 and was written at Gad's Hill Place. It was written at a time of considerable financial insecurity. It was also a time of great personal unhappiness and turbulence, at least partly occasioned by his relationship with Ellen Ternen. Much of the atmosphere of melancholy and menace which dominates the novel comes, no doubt, not only from the marshes which stretched northwards and eastwards from his front door but from his private agonies. There is none of the rather false hilarity which jars on the reader in *Pickwick*, for all its good-natured charm. There is none of the customary Dickensian cockiness. Pip's realisation of his own self-righteousness and snobbery is positively painful.

The marshes, as we have seen, are at the heart of *Great Expectations*. But there is little feeling of the writer's delight in the country which surrounds him. There is certainly a quiet and mature realisation of mortality as he sits near that 'piece of Kentish road . . . a distant river stealing steadily away to the ocean, like a man's life.' (No.XI - 'Tramps' in *The Uncommercial Traveller*) But there is none of that joyous hymn of praise to the countryside which is expressed in the same passage of 'Tramps':

'The road is bordered on either side by a wood, and having on one hand, between the road-dust and the trees, a skirting patch of grass. Wild flowers grow in abundance on this spot, and it lies high and airy . . . To gain the milestone here, which the moss, primroses, violets, blue-bells and wild roses would soon render illegible but for peering travellers pushing them aside with their sticks, you must come up a steep hill, come which way you may.' ('Tramps', same page.)

You would certainly never tell from the novel that the writer has only to look out of the window of the wooden chalet he had built on the other side of the road from the Place.

Here he saw 'the leaves that are quivering at the windows, and the great fields of corn, and the sail dotted river . . . The birds (I wonder if they really did - CW) and the butterflies fly in and out; . . . and the lights and shadows of the clouds come and go with the rest of the company. The scent of the flowers, and indeed everything that is growing for miles and miles is most delicious'. (Quoted by John Oliver in *Dickens' Rochester*, John Hallewell, p.33)

Great Expectations may have been partly written in the library at Gad's Hill Place. But though there is humour and some wit in the novel there is none of the bitter irony which led Dickens to instal dummy book-backs on the back of the library door with titles such as:-

Hansard's Guide to Refreshing Sleep
History of a short Chancery Suit, 21 vols
The Wisdom of our Ancestors - I. Ignorance. II. Superstition. III. The Block. IV. The Stake. V. The Rack. VI. Dirt. VII. Disease and so on.

Nor could you tell from *Great Expectations* - unlike *Pickwick* again, - how Dickens loved to act the host to all and sundry. We would expect him, of course, to entertain with the greatest generosity in his provision of food and drink, though I was surprised to read that Mamie, after her father's death, stated that he himself was 'remarkably abstemious, both in eating and drinking'. (*Dickens at Gad's Hill* p.51) But there is no sign in *Great Expectations* that the author loved to throw the grounds of Gad's Hill Place open to anyone who cared to take part in sports of all kinds, from running and jumping, to cudgelling and boxing.

It was reckoned that on one fine Saturday afternoon 2000 men, women and children walked up the hill from Rochester to Gad's Hill. Sports days were held on part of the 26 acres of meadow and hay at the back of the house, which went with the Place. One enthusiast remembers:-

'Though the landlord of the 'Falstaff' from over the road was allowed to erect a drinking booth, and all the prizes were given in money; though, too, the road from Chatham to Gadshill was like a fair day, and the crowd consisted mainly of rough labouring men, of soldiers and sailors and navvies, there was no disorder, not a flag, rope or stake displaced, and no drunkeness, whatever.'
(J A Nicklin, *Dicken's Land*, quoted Oliver op.cit. p.18)

On one such occasion Dickens recalled a hurdle race. 'One man who came in second ran 120 yards and leaped over ten hurdles with a pipe in his mouth and smoking all the time. 'If it hadn't been for your pipe,' said the Master of Gadshill Place 'you would have been first.' 'I beg your pardon, sir' he answered 'but if it hadn't been for my pipe I should have been nowhere'.' (Quoted Oliver. op.cit. p.64)

Needless to say, Dickens presented the prizes and made a speech at the end of the day.

Then there were the cricket matches held in the hay field, always kept clear for them. Dickens loved to act as scorer. One of his daughters' boyfriends, Percy Fitzgerald, recalls:

'A cricket match - the Higham Eleven against some other competitors - which . . . Dickens treated with a grave solemnity that was amusing and enjoyed the proceedings heartily. There was the umpire's marquee pitched, chairs arranged, flags flying . . . Our host himself officiated as marker (scorer), I see him in his white jean coat, and his grey hat set a little on one side, his double glasses on, going conscientiously through his work; scoring down 'byes' and 'overs' and runs; at times cheering some indifferent hit with an encouraging 'well run! well run!' This he kept up the whole day. He was partial to marking.' (*Dickens at Gad's Hill* p.50.)

At one cricket match, or so we are told - the story seems unlikely to my sceptical ears - 'a Sergeant of the Guards walked up to Dickens and asked:- 'May I look at you, Sir?'

'Oh yes' replied Dickens . . . 'blushing up to the eyes'. . . The Sergeant gazed intently at him for a minute or so, then stood at attention, gave the military salute, and said 'God bless you, Sir!' He then walked off, and was seen no more.'
(Ackroyd op.cit. p.927.)

The top of Gad's Hill was a usual resting place for tramps, and Dickens liked to pass the time of day with them. He thought of them, as Joe Gargery thought of the convicts, as 'poor, miserable fellow creatures' - not as people to pass by without recognition. They often slept on the highway outside the Place, or even on the edge of its garden. But woe betide any intruder! They were liable to be shot at by the gardener or savaged by an Irish blood-hound named Sultan, who arrived after Dickens had completed *Great Expectations*.

Dickens maintained, like all owners of such dogs, that unless Sultan was provoked he was as gentle as a favourite child. This would not have been the view of a private who was marching by Gad's Hill Place with his company when Sultan dashed out and pulled him down. (Dickens says the private was 'objectionable' but it is hard to see how he could have been, poor man.) Nor would the policemen who were chasing an intruder into Dicken's house on the owner's behalf, have been any more enthusiastic about the hound. Dickens caught him 'as he was in the act of flying at them'. He 'was obliged to hold him round the neck with both arms . . . and call to the Force to vanish in an inglorious manner'. In the end Sultan seized a neighbour's child by the leg, and the gardener was ordered to shoot him. One of the family wrote later:

'The gardener took him as far away from the house as he could to kill him, still we all heard the shot, and I can't tell you how terrible it was.' (Watts op.cit. ps. 56-7.)

Dickens was considerate towards his servants. Probably, as Ackroyd says, he remembered that his grandparents had been in service. He gave each one a meticulous job description and so long as they followed out his instructions to the full he had no complaints. He seems to have enjoyed being at least partly in charge, with Mamie, and Catherine Hogarth, of the domestic arrangements - a job presumably done previously by his wife. Each servant was given, when he left, a signed photograph of The Master. Each servant who was in Dicken's service received 19 guineas in his will.

He was a very practical man, and went the rounds of his house - like the captain of a ship or the matron of a hospital - each morning. He liked then to do little carpentry jobs himself, before starting the day's work. He was horrified when the serving lift, which brought up food, trays, crockery and cutlery from the kitchen to the hall, close to the dining room, 'broke and ran down quickly, smashing the crockery'.

Mrs. Wright, the parlour-maid at the time, recalled that it bruised her arm:

'Mr. Dickens jumped up quickly and said 'Never mind the breakage; is your arm hurt?' As it was painful he immediately applied arnica to the bruise, and gave me a glass of port wine.' (Watts, op.cit. p.59)

The servants have left many other memories of their employer - how he took a cold bath every morning and was always opening windows to let in the fresh air. They remembered how he hated to be called 'Sir' but ordered that 'the flag' (what flag?) must always fly above the Place when he was in residence, as if he was royalty. He mustn't be called 'Grandfather' but 'Venerable'. Above all they remembered how nobody was ever allowed into his study with its neat desk, its pens, pencils, blotter and date calendar, all at the ready. It was locked when he was not in it. This was his work place, the heart of his life. Here he died with mirrors all around him on the walls, according to his instructions.

He made the most careful arrangements for his house-guests. Their rooms had comfortable beds, sofas, and cane-bottomed chairs. They were provided with their own writing tables, with paper and pen and plenty of books. They had a kettle, with cup, saucer, milk, teapot, and tea.

Visitors were also provided with excellent food and wine, especially at dinner, and were virtually forced to take part in after dinner games. These might be card games - whist, or vingt-et-un, - guessing games, memory games and, of course, charades, which Dickens adored. He was a fierce competitor, playing all games, as one of his sons said, 'as if his life depended on his success.' If the guests were largely men, they would play billiards, which Dickens used to say 'brings out the mettle'. There were popular ballads to be sung, though Dickens also enjoyed hearing one of his daughters, or others, play Chopin or Mozart.

Sometimes there was dancing. Mamie remembered how he loved the Sir Roger de Coverley:

'He would insist on the sides keeping up a kind of jig step, . . . clapping his hands to add to the fun, and dancing at the backs of those whose enthusiasm he thought needed rousing.

33

Often there were - for the men - compulsory visits to the smoking room 'where', complained one visitor, 'you must drink more gin punch than was good for you.'

At midnight sharp Dickens would retire to bed. He did not expect his guests also to retire, deputing one of his sons or, in their absence, a male guest to extinguish the gas lights and take care of the sideboard keys.

Most important of all, guests were expected to accompany Dickens on his walks, travelling at his pace. Dickens loved to talk with his guests, as they walked along, and often would be seen waving his arms at them in theatrical gestures. On other afternoons Dickens would lay on outings and picnics to Rochester, Faversham, or Canterbury Cathedral. They were planned down to the last picnic basket. Particular care was to be taken that - nightmare of nightmares - the cork screws should not be lost.

Not every visitor could stand such routines, by day and night. Wilkie Collins used to try and disappear to the library with a cigar. Dickens noted his absence and burst in saying 'None of this - no smoking in the library in day time'. Even in the mornings, when Dickens was always working, visitors too had to work and were expected to bring work with them.

Halfway through his time at Gad's Hill Dickens bought some rough land on the other side of the main road called 'The Wilderness'. (It is now part of the Sir John Falstaff pub.) In it he had the wooden chalet erected, to which I have already referred, where some of his later novels were written - part of *Our Mutual Friend*, for instance and *The Mystery of Edwin Drood*, on which he was engaged on the day before he died. His brother Alfred built a tunnel, connecting the Place with the Wilderness and going under the road, which still survives. The entrance to it has a worn sculpture of the God Pan (or some such Greek deity) erected above it in an attempt to give the dreary tunnel some style. On the day my wife and I were being most informatively conducted around the Place and grounds by the Headmistress of Gad's Hill School which now occupies the building we stopped to peer far more closely into the tunnel. Suddenly a small supple rat slipped down a pipe beside the entrance and in a moment was gone. The rat spoke the authentic language of *Great Expectations* and of its author - not the food, nor the drink, nor the hurdling match, not the benign supervision by the Master as scorer - but a little, scuttling rat, disappearing down a dark and disused tunnel.

A year before Dickens died he entertained an American couple Mr and Mrs James T Fields. His hospitality was as lavish as ever and the company as varied and stimulating. Mrs Field loved it all. But she felt - as surely we must - that all this boisterousness hid an anxious and sometimes desperate inner man. Her final comment showed her perceptiveness and stays in the mind, long after the details of her holiday at Gad's Hill. 'Wonderful the flow of spirits' she mused 'Charles Dickens has for a sad man.'

4

THE HOO PENINSULAR

"WHAT MIGHT BE your opinion of the place?" "A most beastly place. Mudbank, mist, swamp and work; work, swamp, mist and mudbank." (One convict's view of the Hoo Peninsula expressed to another - *Great Expectations*, Chapter 28.)

Dickens may only have lived at Gad's Hill during the latter years of his life but the more I thought about the history of the Hoo Peninsula the more I came to the conclusion that it must have had an influence on his mind from many years earlier. Take, for instance, the establishment of workhouses in accordance with the famous Poor Law of 1834. I have no idea whether Dickens knew of the principles on which the new Hoo Union Workhouse was opened shortly before Christmas - of all times - in December 1836. But they followed so closely the harshest demands of the Act that it is difficult not to conclude that he heard about them in his visits to the Chatham area, or read about them in the local press.

Before the Act there had been several small workhouses scattered over the Peninsular, run along lines which local authorities favoured, and therefore varying in the rigour of their treatment of the inmates in their charge. These were all sad cases - the old, the sick, or the insane.

The Act required that these small workhouses be closed and one big workhouse built instead, along lines which were carefully defined, in order to ensure the necessary grimness which would deter all but the most desperate from applying for help. At the heart of the Act lay the provision that 'out-relief' must end, except for short-term help. 'Out-relief', was the payment of money or other forms of help to those in need - the sick, the old, some children - in their own homes. In future the needy must come into the workhouse for help; unless they did so nothing would be given. Surprisingly the Guardians of the new workhouse at Hoo continued to give help to local people in need in their own homes after their workhouse had opened.

But this proved the limit of their humanity.

The Hoo Union workhouse was to cover the needs of the parishes of All Hallows, Cooling, Grain, High Halstow, Hoo St. Mary, Hoo St. Werburgh and Stoke. Eight guardians were duly elected to administer it. The workhouse was built on Elm Meadow, Hoo, close to the present Hoo Institute and on the road to Strood. (The village is now called Hoo St. Werburgh and the building no longer exists.) It was a substantial brick building, two storey high, accommodated 150 paupers with a severe squash, and cost £2,300.

The Master and Matron - a combined post - were Mr. & Mrs. Chiles. They had been appointed from a number of applicants at a combined salary of £25 a year with soap, candles, and provisions provided 'of the same quality as the paupers'. (This last I find impossible to believe, so notoriously meagre was paupers' food.)

The rules of administration which were enforced in the Hoo Union Workhouse were those which were to make the Victorian poor law famous for its inhumanity throughout the world. They still today in completely different circumstances dominate the minds of older men and women who will go to almost any limits to avoid being placed 'in a home'. Married couples were permanently separated - a rule which alone, justified the popular name of 'bastille' applied to workhouses, and over which even the drafter of the act, Sir Edwin Chadwick, who regarded himself as a social reformer, must have had silent qualms when he woke in the middle of the night. Parents were denied access to their children. Meals, which were to consist chiefly of mixtures of thin gruel, oatmeal, and water, were to be eaten in silence. And no division was to be made among those who were admitted to the workhouse. The insane - and these would be bound to include some violent men and women - the young, the old, and all but the very sick (who were grudgingly allowed admission to the workhouse infirmary) were all herded together in the same dormitories and dining hall.

The most famous of all Dickens' novels - and the most socially and politically influential - was *Oliver Twist*, which began to appear in serial form a few months after the Union Workhouse at Hoo was opened. It is difficult not to conclude that he must have heard of this prison in Elm Meadow, when he pictured little Oliver asking for more. For Oliver's Guardians had . . . 'contracted with the water works to lay on an unlimited supply of water; and with a corn factor to supply periodically small quantities of oatmeal; and issued three meals of thin gruel a day, with an onion twice a week, and half a roll on Sundays'. (*Oliver Twist*) Whatever the act might say, many Poor Law Guardians failed in practice to enforce the most severe of the Act's provisions and Hoo was probably unusual in applying them so quickly and in such loyal detail.

Even Dickens, however, did not portray the master of Oliver's workhouse as a sadist. Yet Chiles' successor James Miles seems to have been just that, for which he was dismissed in 1841. (By this time *Oliver Twist* had been finished and published in final form. Perhaps if Miles had reigned a few years earlier he too would have been immortalised in its pages.) He had been, it appeared, 'in the habit of flogging the children, particularly the girls of the age of 13-14.' His dismissal led the Guardians to amend the punishment rules. From then on corporal punishment must be used as seldom as possible and 'inflicted only on the back and shoulders'. If a girl was beaten the punishment must be carried out under the direction of the Matron and in her presence. Alternative punishments were solitary confinement or 'alterations' of diet. (i.e. semi-starvation?)

The marshes of *Great Expectations* were not just gaunt to observe, and laborious to wade through, suitable only for sheep and cattle. They were the sources of 'marsh fever' - malaria. Children were particularly liable to die of malaria, and they did so in unusually large numbers on the peninsular. The lozenge-shaped tombstones over the children's graves at Cooling and elsewhere are probably memorials not, as was always said at the time, to the dangers of the 'unwholesome air issuing from the neighbouring marshes' (as Ireland put it in his *History of Kent*, published in 1830) but to malaria. Indeed the very word 'malaria' (as Mr MacDougall has pointed out in *The Hoo Peninsula*, p.86) means 'bad air'. But adults too were infected and the result was that Dicken's 'marsh country' was an empty country, in which few people would live, unless they had to. 'Kent, sir - everybody knows Kent - apples, cherries, hops and women' says a character in *The Pickwick Papers*. He wouldn't have said that about the Hoo Peninsula.

Towards the end of the century the farmers began to drain the marshes on the Peninsular. By doing so, they destroyed the malaria - carrying mosquitoes (anopheles) which bred there. By 1900 malaria had died out. But it returned towards the end of the First World War on the Island of Grain. The island was unfortunately chosen as a rehabilitation centre for troops returning from Solonika, many of whom had caught malaria there. Grain still possessed some anophele mosquitoes, and soon, as the result of the soldiers, they were infecting local people again. By the end of 1918 50% of Grain's population was suffering from bouts of malaria. Fortunately the epidemic did not spread outside Grain.

The marshes were regularly sprayed against mosquitoes, and inspected between the wars. This finally wiped out the disease. An order was made to prevent any possible return of malaria. If war came no troops with a record of the disease were to be sent to Grain. As the result of such decisive action no attacks have been reported for seventy years and the Peninsular seems now as heavily populated as the rest of the country. No longer is the area an empty land.

The 'hulks' of *Great Expectations* had been part of marsh life for a hundred years before Dickens wrote his novel. When Pip plucked up his courage, the night after his meeting with the convict in the churchyard, and asked Mrs Joe:

'And please what's Hulks?'

he received the infuriated answer:-

'Hulks are prison-ships, right 'cross th' meshes.'

39

And when Pip persisted and wondered:

'Who's put into prison-ships, and why they're put there?'
he was told, after another explosion about 'this boy. Answer him one question and he'll ask you another directly' that:

'People are put in the Hulks because they murder, and because they rob, and forge, and do all sorts of bad . . .'

In the middle of the eighteenth century, when the Seven Years War with France was over and the Navy knew very well that another might soon start again with the ancient enemy, a number of warships had been moored on the either side of the Medway around Chatham on the southern bank and Upnor Castle on the north. Others were moored at Egypt Bay on the Thames. These ships were 'moth-balled', as we would say, and maintenance crews lived on board them ready to bring them quickly up to the standards of active service, should war come. Most of these went to sea as planned, when war was declared on France in 1792, and so cannot really be thought as Dickens' 'hulks', since they never returned in his lifetime.

But other rotting ships, some, though not all, warships, had also been moored along the banks of the Medway from around 1750 onwards, and these were the original 'hulks'. Some were used as prison-ships, others, according to a contemporary writer, were 'occupied by sixty or seventy families . . . Chimneys of brick are raised from the lower gun deck, which gave them a wholesome appearance of a floating town.' (Samuel Ireland - *Picturesque Views of the Medway*.)

The wars with France which went on from 1792 to 1815, three years after Dickens' birth, produced a large haul of French Prisoners of War. Many of these unfortunates were now crammed into old ships on the Medway of various origins, their masts and much of their super-structure removed. Others were luckier, such as those who were sent to Sissinghurst Castle. On one ship, it was said, a thousand prisoners were jammed, where there was room for only three hundred. The prisoners had little exercise, and were poorly fed. No wonder that many died of malaria, yellow fever, cholera, or typhus ('gaol fever'), cooped up, as they were, like battery hens.

Others, though, escaped. There was a thriving trade among fishermen and other boatmen particularly from Faversham, who ferried the POWs across the Channel, hidden in custom-free bales of wool and cloth - for a fee.

From 1815 onwards the 'hulks' became prison ships and housed the thousands of British criminals condemned to long periods of imprisonment for crimes which today would earn a month's suspended sentence - such as petty thefts. Many of these 'criminals' worked their time in Chatham Dockyard and saved the tax-payer a small fortune. Of these offenders, some were boys aged six to twelve, imprisoned in one of the Upnor 'hulks'.

Some of the prisoners in the 'hulks' were imprisoned there while they waited for a convict ship to carry them to Australia. Magwitch, of course, was one of these men, though in fact transportation had ended by the time Dickens was writing *Great Expectations*. The Australians soon grew weary of becoming a dumping ground for British convicts, many of whom were political activists, who had been campaigning for the right to vote or form a trade union, or Irishmen, engaged in their long struggle for independence. Such men proved difficult to handle, and if they stayed in the colony, after they had served their time, continued to fight for similar rights against the wishes of the Governor and his associates. First New South Wales, then Victoria, and finally Western Australia, in the eighteen fifties, refused to accept any more of Britain's 'cast-offs'.

But the 'hulks' were still acting as prison-ships, when Dickens was engaged in his walks over the Hoo Peninsula from Gad's Hill. Their occupants still worked in the dockyard, and it was not until 1880 that the practice of imprisoning boys in the 'hulk' at Upnor ended. Convicts would have been a common enough sight in the town, as they went to and from work. Pip's account in *Great Expectations* reads as if Dickens too had seen them in Chatham or Rochester, and recoiled from them as no doubt did the rest of the population:

'The great numbers on their backs, as if they were street doors; their coarse mangy ungainly outer surface, as if they were lower animals; their ironed legs, apologetically garlanded with pocket handkerchiefs; and the way in which all present looked at them and kept from them: made them a most disagreeable and degraded spectacle.' (*Great Expectations*)

The hulks were not finally abandoned until, at the end of the nineteenth century, a new prison was built on St Mary's Island, Chatham. Only then could a visitor be certain that one of Magwitch's successors might not pounce on him as he walked the lanes of the Peninsular, demanding that he bring him 'wittles' and a file unless he wanted his throat slit.

Bibliography for 'The Landscape of *Great Expectations*'

Philip MacDougall   *The Hoo Peninsula*
(John Hallewell publications, on which I have leaned heavily, especially in 'Landscape' IV).
John Oliver   *Dickens' Rochester* (Hallewell)
Alan Watts   *Dickens at Gad's Hill* (Elvendon Press)
Many of my facts in 'Landscape' III are drawn from this fascinating little book by the Secretary of the Dickens Fellowship.

John Forster   *Life of Charles Dickens* Vol.II (Everyman)
Michael & Mollie Hardwick *Dickens' England* (Dent)
W Lawrence Gadd   *Great Expectations' Country*
                         (Cecil Palmer, 1929)
Walter Dexter   *Days in Dickens Land* (Methuen, 1933)
Peter Ackroyd   *Dickens* (Sinclair - Stevenson, 1990)

5

SATIS HOUSE, ROCHESTER

I F THE MARSHES dominate the early chapters of *Great Expectations*, Satis House broods over much of the rest. Pip's heady rise into the professional classes starts there, while it is from that 'ruined place' at the end that he and Estella go out, hand in hand, to face a future made deliberately and tantalisingly vague. Its very name is made to sound mysterious on Pip's first day when he asks the infuriating Estella whether the house has more than one name:

'Its other name is Satis; which is Greek, or Latin, or Hebrew or all three - or all one to me - for enough'

'Enough House' said I 'that's a curious name, miss.'

'Yes' she replied 'but it meant more than it said. It meant, when it was given, that whoever had this house, could want nothing else. They must have been easily satisfied in those days, I should think.'

Having given Pip as much of an explanation as she sees fit she adds, typically:

'But don't loiter, boy.'

However much argument there may be about the original of Pip's village, there is general agreement that Restoration House in Crow Lane, Rochester, is the model for Satis House. As one is made so regularly aware, Dickens was an artist and not a guide-book writer. So it comes as no surprise to find Restoration House a mere 200 yards off Rochester High Street, whereas the Satis House, of *Great Expectations*, was a quarter of an hour's drive from 'our market town's' High Street by Mr Pumblechook's chaise cart. When Pip returned to the House

43

towards the end of the book - to become involved in the terrible fire in which Miss Havisham was burnt alive in her bridal dress of many years ago - he passed ruins which were as desolate as those at his destination:

'The best light of the day was gone when I passed along the quiet echoing courts behind the High Street. The nooks of ruin where old monks had once had their refectories and gardens, and where the strong walls were now pressed into the service of humble sheds and stables, were almost as silent as the old monks in their graves. The cathedral chimes had at once a sadder and a more remote sound to me, as I hurried on, avoiding observation, than they had ever had

Restoration House, Rochester
the inspiration for Miss Havisham's Satis House in Great Expectations.

before; so, the swell of the old organ was borne to my ears like funeral music; and the rooks, as they hovered about the gray tower, and swung in the bare high trees of the priory garden, seemed to call to me that the place was changed and that Estella was gone out of it for ever.'

Dickens seems to have been fascinated by the house, though he never entered either it or its garden. No doubt when he was a small boy he peered through its locked iron gate, like Pip. He returned to study the house long and intently, three days before he died, when he was in the middle of *Edwin Drood*. It would probably have played a part in the book, had Dickens lived to finish it.

Even though Restoration House - so called because Charles II is supposed to have spent the night there before he entered London on his birthday (30 May 1660) and restored the British monarchy after Cromwell's Protectorate - is so close to the High Street it seems to have stood by itself when Dickens knew it. And today, though it has recently been done up, and its windows are no longer barred or boarded, there is still something grim and foreboding about its exterior. When I peered through the iron gate one recent April afternoon, I felt as if Pumblechook had rung the bell. Surely soon Estella would be flouncing towards me across the courtyard, jangling her keys.

The house is originally Elizabethan, roughly shaped like a U. The windows are tall and narrow. The porch is rounded, and the pilasters reach the eves. Though the front entrance was no longer guarded by two locked chains, as in Miss Havisham's day, I half expected a window to be thrown open above it and a clear voice demand:

'What name?'

And when Estella reached us, I found myself secretly hoping that the odious Pumblechook would be rebuffed in the manner he so richly deserved, after she had opened the gate.

'Mr Pumblechook was coming in also, when she stopped him with the gate.

'Oh!' she said 'Did you wish to see Miss Havisham?'

'If Miss Havisham wished to see me,' returned Mr Pumblechook, discomfited.

'Ah!' said the girl; 'but you see she don't.'

The grim atmosphere makes its way from the house to the front gate still, as mist emanates from the marshes. It comes from the unrelieved colour of the dark brick work of the house. It comes too from the front wall whose brick is of the same colour. The mean white lines of the window frames form the only break in that brooding brick.

But the scale seemed wrong. The courtyard separating the house from the entrance gate seemed so small. Surely, I said to myself, Estella must have had further to go before she reached the mesmerised Pip than that. I felt the same when I wandered along a path at the side of the house and peered over the wall at the garden. It too was being done up, and builders were working to transform it. In a few month's time it would all be ordered, no doubt, with formal rose-beds and rolled lawns. But now it was easy to imagine the deserted garden where there were 'old melon-frames and cucumber frames . . . which seemed in their decline to have produced a spontaneous growth of weak attempts at pieces of old hats and boots, with now and then a weedy off-shoot into the likeness of a battered saucepan.

There was the rank ruin of cabbage stalks, and one box-tree that had been clipped round long ago, like a pudding. It had a new growth at the top of it, out of shape and of a different colour, as if that part of the pudding had stuck to the saucepan and got burnt.'

Yet the garden seemed to extend no further than the garden of any other well established town house. And where oh where was the disused brewery-yard stretching, with its out-buildings, from the side of the house and garden?

Here there had been 'no pigeons in the dove-cot, no horses in the stable, no pigs in the sty, no malt in the storehouse, no smell of grains and beer in the copper or the vat'.

Here Estella had given Pip 'some bread and meat and a little mug of beer. She put the mug down on the stones of the yard, and gave me the bread and meat without looking at me, as insolently as if I were a dog in disgrace.' Pip felt so humiliated that he looked about him for a place to hide his face in 'and got behind one of the gates in the brewery-lane' and leaned his sleeve against the wall and leaned his forehead on it, and cried.

And here he had fought his fight with young Herbert Pocket, and, in the midst of his bewilderment at the whole proceedings, had knocked him down 'again and again and again, until at last he got a bad fall with the back of his head against the wall'.

But of the brewery-yard there was no sign. Restoration House has now no extension at its side and neither has its garden.

Suitably it was starting to rain so I muttered Pip's lament when, years after these events, he had revisited the ruins of garden and brewery-yard and had walked along the paths where Estella and he had walked and had cried to himself: 'So cold, so lonely, so dreary all!' I made for my car.

As I walked down Crow Lane I suddenly realised why the scale of house, courtyard, and garden had seemed so small. It was as if I had been revisiting a place which I had known well in my childhood, but had not seen since. When one pays such a visit, almost always the distances, which appeared once so considerable, seem puny. So it had been today. Dickens, like all great writers, creates his own unique world, as Graham Greene conjures up his Greeneland. When I peered through the iron gate or over the wall of Restoration House I was doing so not with my eyes but with his. As I heard the bell jangling above me, and delighted in Pumblechook's rebuff, I was not myself. I was looking at the scene through the eyes of 'the very queer small boy'.

1

AN UNUSUAL EDUCATION

IN SEPTEMBER 1938, when I was thirteen, I went to a boys' boarding school - Kingswood School in Bath. When war broke out a year later our buildings were commandeered by the Admiralty. We transferred to another boarding school, Uppingham School in Rutland. I stayed there till the summer of 1943, when I joined the Navy.

Both schools were determined to preserve their separate identities, and with hard work, good will on both sides, and ingenuity they succeeded. By means of skilful time-tabling we were taught in separate classes in Uppingham's classrooms. The school's gymnasium was taken over by Kingswood and became our school dining hall, where all three hundred of us ate three meals a day. As for living and sleeping, we were scattered all over the little town.

Looking back on it now, it becomes obvious that at the time Uppingham must have been severely short of pupils. Twenty or so Kingswood boys lived in boarding houses which were only half-full when we moved into them. Other school buildings were quickly converted for use as common rooms or dormitories, as were some large private houses. Inn-Keepers let off whole floors to us. I myself spent half my time in the best hotel in Uppingham - the Falcon Hotel.

Here again - though we never realised it at the time - the proprietor must have blessed our arrival. We took over three-quarters of his guest rooms, sleeping four, six, or eight to a room. It is difficult to see how he could have kept going without us.

We were almost unbelievably free for boarding school boys. So long as we clocked in to lessons, meals, and bed few questions were asked concerning our whereabouts. In the evenings I used to wander out of 'prep.' with my friends whenever I felt inclined - or could afford it.

I used to spend many happy hours in local pubs from the age of fifteen onwards. Publicans - no doubt, like the proprietor of the Falcon, short of customers - used to let us have a room to ourselves, at the back of their establishments. I vividly remember looking idly through to the public bar one evening, and seeing my housemaster enter with a fellow teacher. The publican tactfully blocked the hatch, while signalling to us with his hand behind his back to 'hop it'. We did so at speed, though we cast longing backward looks, as we did so, at the drinks we had barely started. Such experiences give one a relaxed view of modern concerns about 'under age drinking'.

Our freedom of the town was extended to a freedom of the surrounding countryside. We were allowed bicycles and with them were free to roam considerable distances. The roads were almost empty, the nearest built up area (Corby) was six miles away, and the free time, particularly at week-ends, spacious. On summer Sunday afternoons, for instance, there was a good five hours between lunch and tea.

I grew used to making cycling expeditions, with one or two friends. I liked to visit a friend at Oundle School, which was in fairly comfortable cycling distance. The only problem was his hospitality. His housemaster seemed to regard his boys' studies as out of his bounds. When we arrived we were offered a choice of drinks, and, which impressed me most of all, were asked:- 'Turkish or Virginian?'

I loved to bicycle alone to the local reservoir. I would lie on its banks with a book, and watch the sailing boats. One hot summer Sunday afternoon, on the way back to school, I threw myself, on a sudden impulse, down on the grass verge beside the road. I gazed up into the sky which was pale blue and flaked with little trails of cloud. As I gazed up into it, the sky seemed to spin away from me, further and further, in a deep tunnel which had no end. As I lay there, dizzy with the heat and a vision that seemed to be for ever receding, I was drawn far out of myself, and turned around. Instead of looking up, I was looking down on myself from on high. I saw myself as just a speck in the whole universe, and in the vast stretches of time that preceded my birth and would follow my death. For the only time in my life I had some inkling of what that much used - and to me generally incomprehensible - word 'eternity' might mean.

Sometimes on Sunday afternoons I would explore local churches, with an organ-playing friend. The churches were invariably unlocked and empty. (Evensong would not be said till 6.30 in the summer, by which time we would be long since gone.) We would throw down our bikes by the church's lych-gate and walk, dabbing our sweaty faces with wet handkerchiefs, up the church path. As we pushed open the heavy studded old door, and stumbled down two steps, the church seemed like a still pool of cool water, into which we would plunge with relief. While my friend experimented on the organ, I would explore the tombs and read the memorials. I saw my first chain-mailed Crusader then, his feet crossed on top of his tomb chest, his beloved dog at his feet. Those afternoons gave me an interest in parish churches which has remained with me ever since. It only seems surprising that I never tried brass-rubbing.

During my last year, when I was working for a University scholarship, I was only taught for five periods a week. All the rest of the teaching time I spent in Uppingham School's magnificent Library - all thirty periods of it. Here I learned most of the facts of life from Ovid's *Art of Love* which I discovered on the shelves. My Latin was so poor that I failed Higher Subsidiary - but it was good enough for that translation.

Beauty shrieked at you from the surrounding countryside. I used to love to take a particular walk which lasted around 45 minutes - just time between the end of morning school and lunch. Uppingham town then had hardly any surrounding suburbs and you were in the country within five minutes of ending the last period. The roads formed a triangle, and the walk ended at the dining-hall, which you entered with a freshly stimulated appetite.

There were some hard winters at the beginning of our time and I remember once being overwhelmed by the intensity of the points and flashes of light from the snow, as the bright sun shone on it during my walk. The myriads of light, like thousands of sparklers held above the snow, seemed to me to be symbols of sheer joy. Still when I bathe I like to lie on my back and thrash my legs so that the splashing light dances and shines in the same way against the sky or the roof of the swimming bath. And when I do so, I remember those walks around the Triangle.

That walk, and others like it, are associated in my mind with English lessons, when the Head used to read to us the poems of Gerard Manley Hopkins. It was almost as if he, not Hopkins, had written the poems, as he implored us to:

'Look at the stars! Look, up at the skies!

O look at all the fire-folk sitting in the air!'

(Hopkins - 'The Starlight Night')

or asked us, with the poet:-

'Who can ever hold back beauty?' Pronouncing the word 'Beeooty, Beeoty', and drawing it out of his stomach with his long hand and arm.

Many years later I attended a dinner of an old boy's society - not Kingswood Old Boys but Old Boys of a school where I was then teaching. The Guest Speaker was Stanley Spencer, who had recently painted his great 'Crucifixion' for the school's chapel. Within a few minutes of Spencer starting his speech, his audience grew restive and began muttering amongst themselves. Suddenly the tiny little man with his great round goggle spectacles turned on them, jabbing at them with his index finger:

'Yes!' he cried 'Yes! I know the sort of people *you* are. You think, that God gave us eyes so that we wouldn't bump into each other. Well you're *wrong*, that's what you are, wrong, wrong, wrong!'

And I remembered the cry from that classroom, dusty with chalk:

'. . . My heart in hiding

Stirred for a bird - the achieve of, the mastery

of the thing.' (Hopkins - 'The Windhover')

And I remembered that we weren't given eyes just so that we wouldn't bump into each other.

Looking back on those days I can see that the war gave them a particular intensity. I was always aware that school days would soon be over, and that I would then follow my two brothers almost immediately into the forces. (And this, in fact, was exactly what occurred. I was called up for the Navy within seven weeks of my leaving KS. One of my brothers was killed at Salerno shortly afterwards, just as two of my Father's brothers were killed at Gallipoli in the First World War, while he survived.) Life might not last long and you must examine every detail of the scene spread out before you while you could, and sample each experience.

I have loved cricket from the time that I could walk. In the summer of 1943 I achieved my ambition and was appointed Captain of Cricket at Kingswood. We had a moderate season, but it ended with a victory - at Stamford School. The game was played shortly after the end of term. It was a still, golden evening. There were 20 minutes of play left, when we captured their last wicket. Nobody, apart from the players, was about. As we walked to the pavilion I picked up the match ball, which was lying abandoned on the outfield, and tossed it to the cricket master, who had been umpiring. I waved goodbye to him - neither of us felt inclined to stay around - and he put it in the pocket of his white coat. Within ten minutes I had changed and left the ground.

I was spending the night with a friend in Nottingham. My main luggage and bike had already been sent home. After a long wait I caught a bus from the Stamford bus station, and switched off almost completely. In time, I became aware that we were beginning to lurch and rattle down hill in the twilight. Despite the black out, the lights of the city came into view below. The street lights formed steady threads between the darkened rows of houses. Late night shop windows and fish and chip shops cast squares of light on the pavements in front of them. The bands of smoke from the factories drifted across the city centre, which was fully lit. Above, the stars from the clear night sky mirrored the lights below. As I looked down on the city from the upper deck of my bus, I knew that a part of my life was finished and that another would soon take me over. But for the moment, I was numbed, unable to react to any impression and having no wish to try.

2

MY MASTERPIECE

SOME WEEKS after leaving school, I joined the Royal Navy in September 1943. I was told to report to HMS *Ganges*, a training ship at Shotley, near Ipswich. I joined a draft of boys of similar age at Liverpool Street station. Together we caught a train to Harwich. I was knocked off balance by the way in which my companions swore all the time. Of course, I was used to swearing from school. But I had never previously experienced - nor was I ever really to grow used to - the sheer monotonous amount of swearing. Everyone from Petty Officers of twenty year's service to new recruits like ourselves used two swearwords a sentence. They were the same chiefly sexual words used over and over again. The limit this habit placed and places on any power of describing experience or of forecasting the future - let alone of expressing outrage or joy - has to be experienced to be believed.

We none of us had any idea of what the *Ganges* was. It never occurred to any of us that the ship was on dry land. When we were directed on board a ferry I assumed that we would be joining a ship anchored somewhere in the harbour. By now it was dark. Soon the ferry tied up alongside three flights of stone steps. Black out regulations were still strictly enforced and we could only hear an authoritative voice, telling us to 'climb up them bloody Faith, 'Ope and Charity at the double'. (It wasn't until next day that we learned that these were the names of the steps.)

We did as we were ordered and found ourselves at the Main Gate of what appeared to be a vast barracks. As soon as we had passed through the gate, where a ship's figurehead loomed out of the dark at us, we were caught up in a whirl of urgent demands. We had first to hand over our civilian clothes and to sign a receipt for them. We were then kitted out in naval uniform, moving along a huge counter in our vests and pants. We answered interminable questions in a half daze. 'What's yer religion?' ''Aven't got one, Chief.' 'Aven't got a religion? Of course you have, lad. Put down C of E.' Finally we were given a meal in the canteen, and allocated a hut.

At the end of it all we were too tired to do anything other than climb into a bunk bed. But I do remember wondering if I would be able to sleep in my vest and pants for I was allowed nothing else. It was the first time in my life I had slept without pyjamas. Pyjamas, I gathered without asking, were for officers. I never grew used to sleeping without them. But shortly before I was demobilised, and stationed on a land base at Warrington, I thought it was time to defy class distinctions and anticipate my near future. When I pulled up my pyjama trousers, and buttoned the three buttons of the cotton jacket, I felt I had come home.

A Leading Seaman went the rounds of our hut shortly before 'lights out'. As he passed my bed he asked me if I'd seen the mast yet. When I replied that I hadn't he commented grimly: 'You will.' I was too tired to ask him the further questions for which he was hoping and was soon asleep.

the author at 18

When we left the hut next morning to walk over the parade ground for breakfast we saw what he meant. Dominating the vast expanse of asphalt, visible from every part of the barracks, was the mast of the old *Ganges*, a three-decker, built at the time of Trafalgar. It was about 150 feet high.

Stretching at right angles to the mainmast were three yard-arms. Half way up the mast was a lower platform, and near the top a higher one. At the very top stood the Button (a little round, wooden platter, just wide enough to stand on.)

The mast was climbed in three stages. In the first the rope ladders stretched from the ground to the lower yard at a gentle angle. From there you could climb a ladder straight up through what was called the Lubber's Hole to the lower platform. It was made clear to us on the first day that we were to be allowed no such cop-out. We had to climb the Elbow, so called because it resembled an elbow flexed at the joint. From that first yard-arm the Elbow's ladders disappeared backwards over your head at an angle of about 45 degrees until they reached the lower platform. To climb onto the Elbow you had to stretch back over your head with your arms, take a firm grip with your hands and hang by them until your feet had found a rung of the Elbow beneath you. Then you could start climbing outwards to the edge of the lower platform. From there you climbed straight to the upper platform. This was as far as you had to go. Then you descended the rigging on the other side to the lower platform. Here again you had to hang by your hands until your feet gripped a rung below on the Elbow, stretching away underneath you at 45 degrees. By this time your hands had been cut by the rope ladders and were smarting with sweat. It was an easy climb down to the ground once you had managed the descent down the elbow.

I never knew anyone climb to the Button and stand there, but I recently came across a photograph showing a sailor upright on it, saluting. He must have been a steeple jack in civilian life or a licensed nutter.

Underneath the mast was slung a safety net. Apparently this had been installed after a boy had fallen to his death, years earlier. (Recently I read an account of the tragedy which occurred in 1928 in Kenneth Poolman's *The British Sailor*, which prints the photograph I've just mentioned.)

We were told that we would have to climb the mast in 8 weeks' time - half way through the course. Nobody would be exempt.

I had always had a fear of heights and for the next two months I could think only of the Mast. The simple fact that everyone would climb the mast, and that no one would bolt through the Lubbers' Hole, did more to conquer my fear than anything else. We were advised to try ourselves out in stages, and go quietly by ourselves at weekends or in the dinner hour to do so.

It was the Elbow, of course, which dominated our thoughts. The first time when, all by myself, I forced myself to lean backwards and grip the ladder with my hands at full stretch above my head was the most frightening experience of my life before or since. As I launched my feet outwards into space the sky seemed to take a great lurch. Only our instructor's one command 'Never look down, lad. Never look down', which went ringing through my ears, stopped me from looking down at my feet and at the ground below. But I do remember half glimpsing men walking unconcernedly across the parade ground, unaware of my private agony, and being vaguely shocked at their apparent callousness. At last my feet found a hold and I began to climb up and out. The ladder swayed in and out in the wind, though this wasn't visible from below.

When I reached the lower platform I hauled myself by my tummy onto it by the brass rail. I sat there, gasping, with the skies still wheeling around me. I looked straight out to the estuary, where the sun was catching the white sails of the yachts and dancing spots of light off the waves. The sight, which was at eye level and did not call for looking down, steadied me - as did the knowledge that I couldn't sit there indefinitely. I might as well climb up to the higher platform and over now, having got so far.

The descent the other side was just as difficult, but somehow it didn't seem so. Once again the Elbow dominated everything. Again you had to hang from the Platform's rail, while your feet tucked themselves in below. But the worst horror had been overcome.

I had practised the climb so often that the test itself, as we climbed the mast in threes, proved something of an anti-climax. Along with the rest of the draft I climbed *Ganges'* mast and descended without incident. Little notice was taken of our achievement, though the Instructor did say to each batch quietly; 'Well done, lads.' It was expected and it was done. But I still think it was the most difficult achievement of my life. I certainly can remember nothing else about the course except that mast.

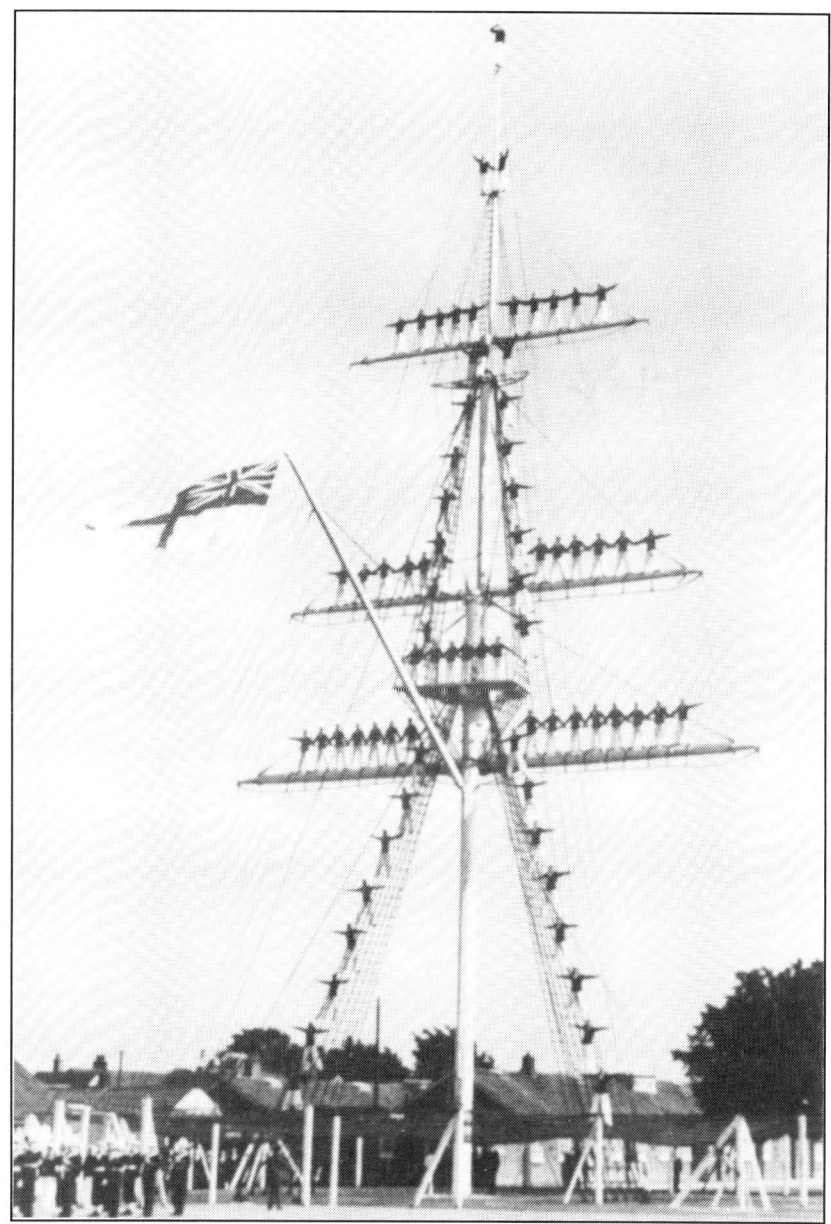

Manning the mast at HMS Ganges

The four months at *Ganges* were meant to lead on to a course for a Commission, but I failed it and was sent to sea as an able-seaman for the next three years in the North Sea, Atlantic and Pacific. Despite the installation of radar, sailors still kept a look-out in the crow's-nests of their ships' main masts. Here you would sit, lashed into a canvas seat, peering with binoculars through the spray and the rain, riding, falling, and rolling with the waves. After the *Ganges* experience all such duties seemed to me pleasantly tame. I used to volunteer for them, and used to enjoy climbing the mast with a cup of cocoa for a mate on duty above in one hand. It never occurred to me that I might slip and fall. Such fears were behind me. But today they still recur occasionally in dreams. I am there on the first yard-arm, stretching back with my hands high above my head, so that I can hang in space from the rungs of the Elbow, while my feet scrabble for a secure foot hold below.

3

ROYAL NAVAL BARRACKS, CHATHAM

I HAPPENED to be in Chatham recently and, on impulse, decided to follow the signs to the old Naval Barracks. It wasn't until I was driving up the hill to the Barracks, with the long high wall on my left, that I realised what I was doing. I had come to lay a ghost.

I had joined the Navy at the height of the second world war, and Chatham was my base. I was a 'Chatham rating' - Able Seaman Wright, C/JX 406204. Along with thousands of others I returned to Chatham when I left a ship for some reason or other, and waited for another posting. For all its traditional language of the sea, its talk of 'going ashore', 'mess-decks', 'port holes' and 'hands to dinner', it was a transit camp, and an extremely crowded one.

The gatehouse, where duty guards and naval police had once stood so threateningly, scrutinising all those who came and went with professional suspicion, was still there. But no one took any notice of me as I walked past it. A man was peacefully painting one of its walls. It seems to belong now to a body called the Kent Export Centre. It was hard to believe that it was here that I had lived through the terrifying experience which now came surging back into my mind.

In February 1945 I was posted to sea after six weeks in Chatham Barracks. The war in Europe was ending, and the great shift of men from Europe to the Pacific was beginning. I was to join an aircraft carrier, 'The Victorious,' and to wait for her in Sydney. Leave was never allowed for those about to sail the next day, but I was determined to spend my last night at home, which was at Marden, in the Weald of Kent.

So I borrowed a friend's identity book and, in the language of the service, 'went ashore'. The penalties for impersonation were severe - thirty days in 'jankers', the naval gaol, where the men of Nelson's Fleet might well have felt at home. But the chances of success were reckoned at ten to one. The population of the Barracks was not only very large. It was for ever on the move. It was hardly surprising that the guards knew few of the faces that were lined up before them, while the Officer of the Watch knew less.

So there I stood, all those years ago, where now the painter was lighting his cigarette, rigid at attention, false identity book held out for inspection on top of my sailor's cap. The officer of the watch, with his accompanying retinue, walked slowly along the ranks. He stopped, as I had seen him do so often, about once every ten men, and compared faces with photographs. He stopped at my neighbour, looked closely at his face and then at his photograph, and moved on. He seemed vaguely interested in my boots, but must have been happy with their polish, for he walked slowly past me and along the line.

My last night with my parents was hardly worth such anxieties. I was sufficiently controlled not to tell them how I came to be at home, but my thoughts were now obsessed with my return to Barracks next morning.

I slept little, and at five the next morning left Marden in a neighbour's car for Maidstone Bus Station. It was still dark when I walked from the Barracks bus stop to the first sentry box. I kept on reminding myself how sleepy the dawn guards were bound to be, and how high were my chances of success, so long as I showed no unusual concern. Small particles of rain were driven by the wind like grit into my face.

The guards were scrutinising the returning libertymen by the light which shone from the guard room, but they were not carrying out individual checks, in the manner of last night. They had picked one man out for questioning. I remember thinking that this was as good a definition of hell as one could compose what with the cold, the driving wind, the dawn twilight and the corrosive fear. I set my face, and marched into the barracks. Nobody stopped me.

But now I made a point of strolling rather than walking up the slope to a new check point. The old barracks buildings are now controlled either by the National Resources Institute or the University of Greenwich. The security man at the first check point represented the Institute, and was amused at my wish to wander around my old haunts. Apart from pointing out to me that virtually everything had changed since the old naval days, he directed me to my old mess block, Anson Block, and left me to walk along Central Avenue. On the face of it, the changes were not as great as he had outlined. There on the right were the grim red brick Victorian mess blocks Hawke, Nelson, Anson, and Grenville. Down below was the parade ground and below it the Dockyard. I made for Anson block where I had been quartered, and where a man from the Institute expected me.

It was here we had lived, sixty to a mess, in high anonymous rooms, designed to take ten. Here too we slept, our hammocks slung from bars which ran across the room. Here we stowed our kit-bags, which contained all our belongings, here we spent all our interminable spare-time, and here we were a prey to theft, or, more commonly, to fears of theft.

For we were all part of an ever shifting company, camped in this room for weeks or sometimes months. Men arrived and departed by night as well as by day, knocking the rows of hammocks as they came and went, which ran into each other along the line like cars driving bumper to bumper, and all along the ranks the sleepy swear words sounded through the dark like the noise of disturbed fowls in a broiler-house. The loyalty and closeness which typified a ship's mess and made it possible to leave a full wallet on the mess-table in safety were here completely absent. Nothing could be left lying around. You kept your money on your person by day, and at night tucked it under your pillow, or stowed it in the pocket of the belt which you were careful never to take off.

The moment, though, I entered the block I saw what my security guard meant. Nothing was left of the old mess-rooms or the stone stairs that led to them, or the high ceilings that loomed above them. The whole block was now composed of offices. I thanked my host from the Institute for his time, and went back outside to continue my walk along Central Avenue.

And now again the past came back. For the essence of Chatham life had been that there was nothing to do. Nothing. Nothing at all. Yet it was a serious offence to stay in your mess, and when the order came after breakfast 'Clear all messdecks' you left to do . . . nothing. But though there were no duties - once you found some you became one of the barrack's permanent staff and here you lasted out the war, the height of many men's ambition - you must never be detected either skiving or loitering. So you soon learnt to look busy.

Along Central Avenue you would walk to study the list of postings for the fifteenth time in a morning, or into the stores to join the queue for slops (clothing), breaking off just when you reached its head to rejoin its rear, nipping crazily behind the great coke-heaps for a drag. The barracks evolved its own myths of men who never stopped walking, and were to be found, still striding out, hammock on shoulder, at three in the morning. They extended inevitably to ghosts, who were half believed to beat the same bounds for ever haunting the trail from football pitch to guard room each night and along the upper road. Certainly I slept close to a man who claimed - he had a girl in town - that he walked out of the mess each morning, hoisted his kitbag on his shoulder as if he had just joined the barracks and kept up a steady pace along the Avenue, each day, every day. 'The thing is, baron, me old friend' he told me once. (Like all ex-public schoolboys who weren't commissioned I was called 'baron' wherever I went in the service). 'You've got to keep moving. So long as you do that they can't touch you.' Did he keep going to the end of the war and did he marry the local girl for whose sake he must have walked more miles in the course of a month than anyone since Napoleon's retreat from Moscow? I will never know though I must admit I like to think of him retracing his steps on Navy Days and showing his children the scene of his old struggles.

At the end of the Avenue I came to the University of Greenwich, and its sphere of influence. Although I could see no sign of them, I was particularly concerned to see again the grove of statues that stood at the end of the parade ground and which, if they still stood, would do so on the University's patch. I used to love to walk at a brisk pace down here, keeping moving in the approved manner, to study this roll call of the glorious dead. One statue in particular used to strike my eye - that of Richard Parker.

Lieut. Parker had been the leader of the most serious mutiny the navy had ever known, that in 1797. He had persuaded the Chatham sailors that they should no longer endure in silence the cruel floggings, the miserable pay, and the all but uneatable food. He had called on them to do the unthinkable and refuse to set sail to fight the French, and they had followed him. The mutiny, of course, had collapsed and Parker had paid for his courage in the traditional way. Before an audience of sailors paraded on the decks of their ships, anchored around the flag-ship HMS *Sandwich*, and in sight of the crowds assembled on the nearby Isle of Grain, Parker had been hanged from the yard arm and his body had been left dangling in the wind as an example to others.

What on earth had persuaded their Lordships of the Admiralty to include Parker amongst that line of the great, along with Collingwood, Howard, Blake, and Nelson? Was it a long overdue sense of justice, or a supreme example of British hypocrisy to add Parker to that line of glorious dead? Something of both, perhaps.

The man on the gate at the entrance to the University's territory raised no objection to my search of the area where once the statues had stood. But of course, I could find no trace of them. As I was walking the road I was stopped and questioned (in the politest possible way) by a security guard in a patrol car. Though he seemed quickly satisfied of my innocence, he followed me - and then returned - to make sure that my activities were harmless. I was left wondering why the National Resources Institute and the University of Greenwich need security men at all. Is it just a throw back to wartime - or does some secret work of national importance continue?

Whatever the reason, the Naval Barracks still had about it a feel of the old menace, just enough to make me deeply thankful, as I drove past the old gate house and waved at the painter, that I would never again be Able Seaman Wright, C/JX 406204.

4

SOME THOUGHTS
on WORST CASE SCENARIOS

I AM ALWAYS SHY of talking about my experiences in the Second World War, though recently I have grown more confident. I am the youngest of three brothers. One of them, an Army Captain, was killed in Italy shortly after the Allied landing at Salerno. He was awarded the DSO for great bravery, an award rarely given to junior officers. He went out with a party into 'no man's land' to rescue one of his men and was killed in the attempt. The other was a navigating officer in the RAF who won the DFC for similar courage. Neither was in the regular services. My experiences as an Able-Seaman in the Royal Navy form a tale which is hardly worth telling in such company. Yet my time in the Navy was remarkable in one way. I was involved in four actions which were regarded then - as they are now - as some of the most dangerous naval actions of the war. Yet I never once saw a shot fired in anger.

For nine months, from January 1944, I was an Able-Seaman on board HMS *Nairana*, an aircraft carrier converted from an old merchant ship. At first we formed part of an escort convoy which also included destroyers, frigates and corvettes. Our job was to escort oil tankers and merchant ships carrying goods of all sorts from the Firth of Clyde to Gibraltar.

Swordfish aircraft, flying from our flight deck, patrolled the seas around the convoy, where U-boat packs trailed us, often in large numbers. For the Battle of the Atlantic had not yet been won. The Germans remained confident that their U-boats could limit and eventually stop the passage of ships carrying goods across the Atlantic to Britain and the convoys from Britain to the Mediterranean. Their bases in Brittany and along the French Atlantic coast enabled their submarines, with steadily improving technology, to range far across the North Atlantic. Their submarine commanders formed a brave and highly trained élite, and I have a vivid personal memory of a U-boat's crew, with whom I came in contact. They had been captured at Sea a few weeks previously and taken by a destroyer to Gibraltar. Here we picked them up and had to carry them to a POW camp in Britain. They were locked in our ship's cells on the voyage and for a few days I had the job of bringing them their food. They would not even recognise my existence, and did not respond to any smile or gesture of common humanity. I had never been made to feel I didn't exist before, and in the end I just placed the food at the entrance to their cells and went on my way. If such contemptuous defiance is a definition of high morale those men's morale appeared to be high.

During our time on convoy duty in the Atlantic, numbers of British ships, both merchant and naval, were lost in various engagements along with most of their crew. Yet not a single ship, either in our convoys or their escorts, was even slightly damaged on the runs in which we were engaged. Only our air crew suffered and I saw something of their ordeals at close quarters.

I was a 'chock-man'. It was my job to sit on the chocks which propped up the wheels of a Swordfish on the carrier's decks and prevented it pitching or rolling. In the swell and high seas of the Bay of Biscay those decks rolled prodigiously, on occasions as much as 45 degrees. So we would sit on our chocks right up to the moment of take off when the 'batman' would signal to us 'Chocks away' and we would scuttle, grasping our chocks, to safety as the Swordfish began to taxi along the deck.

At night when the carrier was totally blacked out, and the only lights which guided the pilots back to base were the sharp little tips at the ends of the 'batman's' baton, like points of electric light on a Christmas tree, I used to marvel at the skill of the young pilots. Somehow they would find their way back to us in the dark, and land on the pitching, rolling decks. We would crouch on the edges of the

66

decks with our chocks, and at the signal, dash forward, heads low, to avoid being sucked in by the planes' propellers, and wedge the wheels of our Swordfish secure once it had come to rest.

Inevitably, some aircraft would land on the edges of the flight deck, and topple into the churning sea. The Captain allowed the play of searchlights on the water for longer than he probably should have done, but few pilots or gunners were saved. Some of our aircraft, of course, were shot down miles away from home by U-boat guns, or long range planes flying from West French bases, but more were lost in such accidents. I do remember, though, helping to haul a pilot to safety up the scrambling net we had hurriedly thrown over the bucking side of the carrier one black night. Somehow the pilot had managed to climb into his lifeboat, when his Swordfish lunged over the ship's side. He plunged his paddle into the water with desperate strength. Each time after he had risen to the seething, hissing top of the waves and was dropping deep down into the valley the other side, we gave him up for lost. Then when he reappeared, nearer each time to safety, we cheered until at last the hands of his fellow airmen hauled him over the ship's side. During these nine months the convoy was never penetrated, nor were any of its escorts attacked.

Apart from the loss of these aircraft one of my main memories of those days at sea is of the sheer joy of off-duty times on deck, when I would just sit (weather permitting) and observe the scene around us as we drove our way through the Bay, our pace that of the slowest merchant ship, towards Gibraltar. For despite all the gloomy prophecies, I was never sea-sick, nor was I ever anywhere near that debilitating state. Nor, may I say, was any of the crew to the best of my observation. Probably this was because we were kept constantly hard at work and told that even if we were sick, we would have to continue just the same.

I used to love most of all leaning over the carrier's bows and watching the porpoises play in front of them. They would lie back, as if to look at us, and then dash off behind us, their sleek black bodies arching in and out of the white frothy water. Then they would be back again at our bows, for all the world as if they were saying: 'Come on! Can't you go faster than that for heaven's sake? Look at me! You can't catch me!'

In June 1944 we formed part of a large naval force which was ordered to seal off the entrance to the Channel from Cornwall to Brittany. Our job - and that of our patrolling aircraft - was to prevent any U-boat entering the Western Approaches to the Channel and attacking the ships carrying men and supplies to the Normandy beaches. Now surely, we thought, with the sort of anticipatory fear which contains pleasure as well as pain, this time we will be for it. Every available U-boat will be at sea to prevent this, the decisive landing. Probably numbers of German surface vessels too, operating from nearby French bases, will put in an appearance. If we survive torpedo attacks by sea we will be dive-bombed by Heinkels and Messerschmidts from the air. Had they not, four years earlier, at the time of Dunkirk, succeeded in driving the British Navy out of the Eastern approaches to the Channel altogether? In the event nothing happened. So far as I know no U-boat penetrated our screen, and certainly we never saw an enemy aircraft. In fact I had more leisure in which to read newspapers, which were flown regularly aboard from Britain, and books which were on the reading-list given to me as preparation for the first year university course which awaited me on demobilisation, than at any other period of the war.

In the autumn of 1944 we were ordered to Scapa Flow, the great naval base off the North of Scotland. It became known that we were to form part of the escort protecting the next Russian convoy. Once again - and with very good reason - we feared for our future. For two years losses of naval and merchant ships carrying goods -particularly tanks and oil - to Murmansk had been notoriously high. German planes and U-boats, even German surface ships, operating from North Norwegian bases, could pick off ships taking supplies to the Russians, together with their protection vessels, almost at will as they rounded the North Cape of Norway. After all, allied ships had to sail within 20 miles of the enemy coast. This time -we told ourselves - we really were for it. Few men survived more than 15 minutes in those Arctic waters.

But the outward journey proved uneventful. We were sailing through seas made mountainous by the autumn gales, and I used to be mesmerised at the progress of a small British Landing Craft, flying the Soviet flag, which was stationed near us at the centre of the convoy. She would dip deep into the great seas, as if sliding down a steep waterfall, so deeply that over and over again we gave her up as lost. 'This time' we would say 'This time surely she's had it.' Yet there she was again, bobbing along on the crest of the next vast wave, before sliding down the next mountain slope into the boiling cauldrons below.

When we reached Murmansk harbour the little landing craft anchored next to us. In accordance with Royal Naval protocol, the captain's motor launch was despatched to the craft, our nearest vessel, with an invitation to her skipper to join our Captain for drinks in the wardroom. I formed part of the reception party, which saluted and blew the traditional high wailing notes on our naval pipes, as the launch carrying the Russian Captain approached our gangway. (We had been polishing our boots and whitening our caps and lanyards for days beforehand.) As the Russian captain began to mount the gangway steps, our Captain, dressed in full ceremonial uniform, his medal ribbons pressed to perfection, exploded so that all could hear his cry. 'Good God!' he shouted 'It's a woman!'

The Captain had warned us that we were in the greatest danger during the 24 hours immediately after we left Murmansk harbour to start the journey home - the hours when we were closest to the Cape. The Germans would be bound to know exactly when we left harbour. So we were not surprised to be called to 'Action Stations' shortly after we had weighed anchor. A Petty Officer Coxswain and I were stationed in the ship's bows, ready to man the emergency steering wheel. Should the main steering fail, we would have to take over under direction from the bridge.

We sat in a self-contained compartment below the waterline and behind water-tight doors. If the bows were hit, and we were ordered to leave our station as water poured into it, it was absolutely essential that we seal our station behind us so that the rest of the ship was not flooded. This would mean first undoing and then sealing up those doors behind us, perhaps against the weight of advancing water. This was a cumbrous and time consuming process, which we had practised, but which I dreaded, since the handles were stiff and, like the doors, heavy.

Shortly after taking up our station the Captain's shrill voice came over the Tannoy: 'Attention, all hands! Attention all hands! Torpedo sighted travelling towards our bows. Torpedo sighted travelling towards our bows. Close up and be ready to operate emergency procedures! Close up and be ready . . .' The two of us sat waiting for the worst to happen, and I suppose had every reason to think that in some form or other it might.

I was later struck by the fatuously optimistic and inadequate nature of my reactions. Not for me the feelings of which one reads - that men facing death are given a deeper insight into the very meaning of life itself, or that they are suddenly filled with a new and purposeful energy. My first reaction was one of plain incredulity. 'This can't be happening to me - not to me!' The second was of what, today, would be called alienation. 'This isn't really happening at all, or at least if it is I'm not engaged in it. I'm watching it happen from somewhere outside and above myself.'

We stayed in a state of expectancy for about a quarter of an hour. Then the Captain announced in a rather sheepish manner that whatever the cause of the danger it had now passed. We returned to normal, and indeed returned to Scapa without losing a man, the first Russian convoy to do so.

When we were back I was sent on a navigational course. A few months later I saw a photograph of the *Nairana* on the front page of a newspaper. She was travelling through high seas, her bows wreathed in spray. Alongside the photo was an account of a recent Russian convoy from which she had just returned. Losses of ships and planes had been heavy. In some of the worst weather ever known off the North Cape numbers of aircraft and men had been lost taking off or landing on the carrier's decks, which sloped as high as 45 degrees.

In the Spring of 1945 I was sent to Sydney to join the aircraft carrier, the *Victorious*. I joined her shortly before VE Day. She had recently been hit directly on her bows by two Kamikaze planes. The pilots had dropped their planes, with, of course, themselves inside them, from a great height directly on the carrier's flight deck. The deck still showed two great dents, and it was extraordinary and a tribute to those who had built the *Victorious* that only eight of the ship's crew had been killed.

This seemed to me a foretaste of what was to come. Like most of my new shipmates I was left feeling rather scratchy by the VE Day jollifications. There didn't seem much to celebrate for us as we sailed North, part of the British Pacific Fleet, due to rendezvous sixty miles off the Japanese coast with the vast American Fleet. When we reached the spot American ships stretched as far as the eye could see and much further in the clear Pacific light. Surely, when we sailed close to the Japanese homeland, more than two Kamikaze planes would be screaming out of the sky, to land close to the Bridge, where I worked now as yeoman - or secretary - to the Navigation Officer.

For a month or so our and American planes flew over Japan, retiring and returning at three-day intervals. It was repeatedly made clear to us - positively gloatingly I thought - that there was little chance of the Japs surrendering before Christmas 1946. During this month we lost some planes, but no Japanese ships or pilots penetrated the convoy's defences. Mail and newspapers were delivered to us, often a mere 5 days after they had been posted in the UK. I have never before or since read the *Times* from cover to cover. My thoughtful Father had sent me its airmail edition when I left England, and I covered the course of the sensational 1945 General Election in considerable detail as we cruised off Japan and rejoiced at its unexpected result. One of my most magical memories is of the schools of flying fish - we fried some for breakfast, hardly worth doing, so little flesh do they contain - which landed and lay blue-back on deck. At night I would sling my hammock in the open air and gaze up at the stars which were shining more brightly than any stars I had ever seen. Lulled to sleep by the gentle motion of the ship I spent some of the best, though some of the shortest, nights of my life.

Then, early in August, someone in our mess picked up a news flash on a mess radio. It talked about the dropping of a super-bomb on the Japanese. Within a few minutes the loudspeakers called:- 'All hands assemble on the flight deck!'

Here the Captain harangued us. We were to take no notice of rumours about fancy sorts of bombs. Never mind what sort of invention the 'boffins' came up with. He repeated the word several times with satisfaction. Wars were won with human courage - and cold steel. Make no mistake about it. The Jap would fight to the last man, as he had in Iwojima or Okinawa. There was no chance of our returning home before Christmas 1946 - no chance whatsoever. We must put all other ideas out of our minds.

A few days later the Tannoy went again to call all hands to the flight deck. The Captain announced the end of the war without comment, and called on the Chaplain to lead us in a service of thanksgiving.

Experiences such as these have left me dangerously complacent. I have grown used to believing, deep down, that in great international crises in which Britain is involved the worst simply will not happen. The years since August 1945 have appeared to justify my complacency and made it worse. Hungary, Suez, Berlin, Czechoslovakia, President Reagan's 'evil Empire' speech, above all, Cuba . . . Each has threatened destruction on an unimaginable scale. Terrible suffering - almost certainly death - have stared us in the face. Yet the worst has not happened, and our lives in Britain have continued undisturbed.

There is nothing whatsoever to be proud of in such reactions. Not only can I be fairly accused of complacency. I am almost certainly dangerously out of date. I, and the hundreds of thousands of people like me, may be prisoners of an irrelevant past. Our memories of past survivals may lead us to underestimate present dangers. I can only record the fact that faced with imminent dangers which appear to threaten appalling suffering on hundreds of thousands of people my gut reaction is to say: 'It won't happen and if it does it won't be as bad as you're making out.' This is a position which is neither realistic nor honourable. But I comfort myself with the thought that perhaps it is better than to become one more prophet of doom.

5

THE SOUP RUN

FOR THE LAST few years the local Council of Churches has organised a 'soup-run' in Canterbury. Each night volunteers from the duty church set up a stall. Here for about an hour they serve soup, tea, coffee and sandwiches to any homeless or otherwise destitute people who come. Sometimes there are ten, sometimes twenty-five.

Two years ago I joined the volunteers. I went first with men and women from the local Roman Catholic Church. Later I joined Salvation Army Officers, whose turn fell on Friday evenings. Each time I set off with feelings of incredulity mixed with shame at what I was doing. For years I used to teach my history classes about the Victorian 'soup kitchen', that symbol of the Victorian class system. Always I did so, I suppose, with a hidden air of superiority. For those were the bad old days, which I assumed would never return. Now here I was, engaged on the same operation.

I have seen some nasty incidents though I have never heard of a volunteer being harmed. Once two young men - nobody knew whether they were associated with the little group gathered round the stall or not - drove their car fast through the window of the Electricity Board's show room nearby. They backed with a squealing of brakes and were off before I knew what had happened. Another time a young man rushed up, arguing fiercely with a girl. When she swore at him he hurled her against a brick wall breaking, as we were later told, her collar bone. On another occasion a young man had run up to us, blood streaming from a cut between his eyes, saying he was being chased. The Officer produced some cotton wool, but he was gone before she could mop him up. And then there was the night of the roaring drunk and the girl straight out of public school.

The drunk was a regular - a middle-aged Irishman, with a bellow like a ship in distress. He was generally there before we came, at our pitch beneath the multi-storey car park. He was there this time when we arrived, swaying, roaring out 'Where have you been?' and brandishing a half empty bottle of British Sherry. (It was always British Sherry.) His conversation always followed the same track. We called ourselves Christians, did we? Well we weren't true . . . (he prolonged the adjective until I thought the sentence would just fade away) Christians. The only true . . . Christians were people like himself. They helped people who needed it. Once I grew annoyed and asked him what he thought we were doing there. He flew into a rage and I vowed never to react in that way again.

This time he sat slumped against the wall behind the stall and began running his hands up the Officer's skirts. In the end she told him that next time he did that she would slap his face. After that he left her alone and latched on to me. He thrust his face close to mine, his rheumy eyes within inches of my own. He was as filthy as ever, his hands clenched in woollen gloves caked in dirt, his heavy boots crusted with clay soil, his face blotched with lumps of mud. We swayed precariously together, led by his mood of general benevolence. Soon he collapsed on the rain-soaked pavement and crawled under the car park stairs. Here he lay, still clutching his bottle of British Sherry. I forgot about him and went on serving tea and coffee. We were busy that night.

Suddenly a tall girl, elegantly dressed and draped in a poncho, walked quickly up to us. She asked for tea in a Roedean voice. She was joined by another nineteen year old who spoke polite, impeccable English in a slightly German accent. The damp nose of a young puppy peeped out of the top of the German girl's expensive anorak.

They had joined us well after 9pm. When we began packing up, the two girls wandered off to where British Sherry was lying on the pavement. Suddenly they were joined by a young man, who came from nowhere, dirty, wet, with a face layered with mud. The German girl and he recognised each other instantly, and began passionately embracing. All of a sudden British Sherry sat up, saw Roedean, hurled himself to his feet, and threw his arms around her to her exuberant delight. When we drove off the four were still in the same place, an indistinguishable lump of humanity, swaying in their embraces, like a bush planted on the glistening pavement, responding to the night winds - an image perhaps of Mr Major's classless society.

Next week I picked up the Sally Army Officer in my car, and drove with the urns and sandwiches to the stall. There was the usual urn of vegetable soup, another of hot water for tea and coffee, and more sandwiches than were eaten, though the dogs, who accompanied so many of the customers, did well too.

At first not many came. Of the old quartet only the German girl was there, now very drunk. When I pressed a cup of tea on her she waved a can of beer and said 'I prefer this.' A well dressed middle-aged man began a long theological discussion with me. He had the voice and vocabulary of an academic, and had been sampling the local churches. The conversation grew stranger and stranger. Finally, he lost me when he told me how God answers prayers. After your prayer is ended, he said, you must listen to the next noise that you hear. If a dog, for instance, barks once or somebody coughs, then God is saying 'Yes.' If twice, 'No.' He glanced at me and said 'You look sceptical.' I had to agree that I was and left him as soon as seemed kindly.

By now about a dozen people had come up to us. I approached a little group under the stairs, huddled in the dark. A young man and a young woman were bending over a sixteen year old girl, with rings in her nostrils. She had come earlier to the stall and I had been struck then by her face which was white as death. She was having a fit of some sort and the two were holding her tight. I bent down to the pavement to look more closely, but was waved away. They were used to her. She would be all right. They would look after her. She looked in a terrible state to me and I told the Salvation Army Officer about her. She proved no more successful than I had been. Soon the young man picked her up, and lifted her over his shoulder, holding her as closely as he could. The woman threw a blanket over her and the three of them staggered off into the night. They seemed to have decided to make tracks when the Officer told them the girl should be taken to hospital. 'It's always the same with drug cases,' the officer said 'they won't go near a hospital.'

The evening was enlivened by the arrival of a young Scotsman, dressed in a flowered shirt, and wearing a top hat which had grown soggy with rain. He took four rubber balls from his shirt and began to juggle with them.

A girl was helping us at the stall. Her eyes lit up when she saw the juggling, and she persuaded the Scotsman to let her join him in a double act. The two meshed well together. (He was the better juggler, but she hadn't been drinking.) Then he produced four clubs and began flame-throwing, while the girl took a break. The red and yellow flames rose high against the shop windows, which reflected their long plumes. They looked like the wings of tropical birds. But the drink proved too much for him, though he managed to light his cigarette from the flames somehow, without burning his cheeks. When he dropped first one and then another club he put out the fire and came for a coffee.

When the clubs had cooled, the girl joined him and they began throwing them to each other and juggling the balls. Clubs and balls rose higher and higher and fell out of the shafts of light which shone between the concrete stairs and grimy pillars. The filthy little group of men and dogs, sitting slumped on the pavement around the German girl, wrapped in new Salvation Army blankets, wet and dejected, peered through the drizzle at the couple as they grew wilder and wilder. The whole scene formed an image of our times, fit, perhaps, to be set alongside the Victorian soup kitchen.

1

ON THE MAP
a song on the names
of East Kent
villages
by
Martin Child

Chorus   Oh! If I had a fortune then I'd follow you,
        To Majorca the South of France, or Timbuctoo;
        But instead of all that travelling, I'm quite content
        To live in any of the villages of Eastern Kent.

1.   If I were a monarch then I'd give my crown
        For Plucks Gutter or Hackling Holes or Wheelbarrow Town;
        I don't know of any lovelier places on earth
        Than Great and Little Shuttlesfield or Paddlesworth.

2.   If I had no money left I'd have to go
        To live in Mockbeggar, Wallet's Court or Farthingloe;
        But instead I'll thank the Lord for the food I've got
        And stay in Plumpudding Island, Ham or Honeypot.

3.   If I wanted to give another country a glance
        I'd go to Dunkirk, Gibraltar or Petty France;
        Or if I felt like travelling a bit further than that
        There's always Bethlehem, Mount Ephraim or Mount Ararat.

4. If I went to Paramour Street, I'd soon go on
    To Heart's Delight, Marriage Farm, and Weddington;
    But if I took to crime and had some time to kill
    I'd visit Knave's Ash and Cop Street and Swingie Hill.

5. If only I had time to visit more of these
    Such as Ripple Staple Crabble Gore or Old Wives Lees;
    Then there's Ottinge Coolinge Geddinge Sellinge
                                    Podlinge Town
    Or simply Twitham Bagham Waterham and Soakham Down.

6. If I were going downhill as fast as I could
    I'd soon reach Knight's Bottom, Oddy Bottom,
                                    River Bottom Wood;
    But if I went too fast, I'd keep a sharp look-out
    For Ratling Rowling Shatterling and Thanington Without.

Chorus Oh! If I had a fortune then I'd follow you,
    To Majorca, the South of France or Timbuctoo;
    But instead of all that travelling, I'm quite content
    To live in any of the villages of Eastern Kent.

2

KENT CRICKET and the
FIRST SUNDAY LEAGUE MATCH

I HAVE ALWAYS been fond of cricket, and saw my first county match at the age of six on the Bat and Ball ground at Gravesend. (Leslie Ames, later manager of the county XI for many years, made a hundred on this occasion. He secured himself in my affections for life by sending me, on request, a signed photograph of his kindly, smiling face.) To a cricket lover in the London area, whose opportunities for watching county cricket had been confined to sitting, huddled with a few fellow spirits, in the great empty amphitheatres of Lords or the Oval, a move to Kent at the end of the sixties came as a lift to the heart. It was an extra bonus that my return to the county of my birth happened to coincide with the arrival of one day cricket.

The moment I entered the St. Lawrence ground at Canterbury for a county match in the summer of 1968 during the lunch interval I felt I had come home. It was the sight of those scores of individual games while the players were having their lunch that turned me back - back to matches I had seen at the Bat and Ball, at Tonbridge, at Dover, and most of all at Mote Park, Maidstone, during the thirties and immediately after the war. I could remember the sensations so well. Always the last thing you checked, when you went over your picnic bag, was the tennis ball. Had you remembered it? (Your bat was under your arm.) So, as the last few balls before lunch were bowled, you edged to the boundary line. As the umpires removed the bails, and the players made thirstily for the pavilion, you dashed after them to form part of the spectators' corridor through which they passed to their dressing room, thrusting out your autograph book. Then you threw down your jacket or jersey, hurled the ball at your brother, and staked out your claim. He started bowling at you at almost exactly the same time as thirty other games got under way, and soon the spectators, who were eating their sandwiches or reading their papers on the rough wooden planks, were throwing back the balls which suddenly bounced among them with the same invariable good humour that characterised their mood all day. Tea saw the same happy, anarchic scene - a nightmare long since banished from Lords and the Oval - and half an hour after stumps were drawn the shrill cries of triumph or more frequently of disputation rang round the empty ring. There it was, that August early afternoon in 1968, almost exactly the same spectacle, and there it can still be seen on any of the lovely Kent grounds, - far fewer, alas!, now - whenever the county XI is playing at home.

But even my romantic childhood memories do not compare for poignancy, relaxed pleasure and excitement with the Sunday League games which started soon after my return to Kent. At these Sunday matches the gates are opened in the morning, and the games between friends or within families will be going from ten or eleven o'clock onwards. From all over the county, and outside it - particularly from the suburbs of south London - the cars converge on the grounds with their packed picnic baskets, transistor radios, colour supplements, optimistically packed sun glasses, and fold-up chairs. Once the car is parked, the long Sunday morning begins. The beer-tents are crowded - there is something particularly agreeable about the damp, cool atmosphere of a large marquee on a warm summer's day, the tang of wet earth mingling with the hot sweet smell of beer - the rugs are out for the Sunday lunch, women are struggling with spirit stoves and wondering furiously where their men have got to, and well before the first ball is bowled at half past one the Kent side is practising. I met an acquaintance of mine who lives in Maidstone. Every Sunday - and that is eight Sundays a summer - when Kent is playing at home he, his wife, and his three young children leave home by ten for Canterbury, or Folkestone, or his local Mote Park, and aim to be settled in for the day, three hours or so before the start of play. What cheaper happiness is there for a boy or girl than Junior membership of the Kent club? For £18 a year he can watch Kent's matches, weekdays, and weekends, six hours a day, and find a pleasure which, if he is anything at all like me, will last him all his life.

In 1969 I missed the first Sunday game at Folkestone, and arrived just in time for the second - against Yorkshire at Canterbury. The press had given the match some advance publicity, partly because there is more than the usual needle in the air whenever Yorkshire - gritty, we are told, no-nonsense,professional Northern - play Kent, soft, southern, amateur. This year it was supposed to be the result of the alleged rivalry between the two captains, Geoffrey Boycott and Michael Denness. The cold was enough to keep all but the most dedicated supporters at home around their Sunday afternoon fires. But the crowd was a good one, though there were more spectators watching from their cars, at start of play, than in the open. The air was like damp flannel, the man in front of me wore a Russian fur hat - the sort made fashionable by Harold Macmillan at the end of the fifties - and the sawdust at the bowlers' run-ups looked like patches of impetigo on the closely shaved face of the grass.

Over the alternate strips of light green and dark green turf the dome of the sky sat like a great steel meat cover. One became incredulously aware that the sun might be trying to filter through.

Yorkshire started well, Boycott, stunning the rising ball, head right over the line. Kent's fielding was as flowing and athletic as ever. The ball was picked up and returned all in one gesture, while the England wicket-keeper, Alan Knott, lived in his usual world of perpetual motion, marching up and down between overs, arms swinging like a guardsman, touching his toes between balls, hugging his arms across his chest to keep warm, signalling for the ball from the boundary fieldsman, with one raised arm. A bump ball thrown up by the bowler in mock excitement produced the roar from the deceived crowd that it always does, a waddling chase to the boundary by the popular ungainly Kent bowler, Norman Graham, was greeted with delighted sarcastic cheers, and the first six of the day landed just short of the cars by the main entrance. Yorkshire seemed well on their way, when suddenly unaccountable calamities struck. To soft-centred Kentishmen the mistakes of the hard men from the North seemed frankly incredible. First Luckhurst plucked a big hit from Hampshire out of the air on the square leg boundary - had he not been stationed there the hit would have scored six - and then the great Boycott appeared to go mad. He charged down the wicket before the ball was bowled - and a sigh of incredulity spread round the ground as the infallible Knott failed to stump him. At the next ball he lunged absurdly, and started walking back to the pavilion, only to return when the catch fell between bowler and fielder, each leaving it to the other like schoolboys. Then, in the very next over, he swung wildly once again, this time to be bowled to the accompaniment of an exultant Kentish roar. We were left, as the Yorkshire innings petered away, to wonder what strange death wish could have entered the man's mind, for without Boycott Yorkshire, at that time, were nothing.

The cricket was temporarily dead, and I made my way to the Pavilion. Here is the secret of Kent's success - democracy. The pavilion at Canterbury, or at any of the other Kent grounds, reveals a scene which is essentially that of the village cricket club writ large. It is overrun with children, mothers, teenage girls, and old followers of Kent Cricket talking of Huish and Hubble. It is reserved for members - though members of all ages - but nobody seems to check the passes very carefully. At the bar old friends are forever meeting. The players mingle with the crowds, and when they go out to field they are touched and slapped, as if the act of contact bestows a blessing or establishes a cure like touching for the Queen's evil. When I first joined the club and entered the pavilion on the St. Lawrence Ground I was used to the Long Room at Lord's where members did not speak unless spoken to, where batsmen passed through from their distant dressing room at the top of the great staircase (new players had to be shown the way out to bat) and went inscrutably to the wicket, where neither women, nor children were allowed. To go from the pavilion at Lord's to that at Canterbury is to pass from the most decorous of London clubs to the world of the village pavilion. I had hardly arrived there when I was hailed by my taxi driver of a few days back, who was making a day of it. I didn't stay long. I wanted to visit the Picture Gallery before the Yorkshire innings ended.

It is a matter of argument whether cricket started first in Hampshire or in Kent. Certainly a visit to the Picture Gallery on the St. Lawrence Ground makes one aware of the length of cricketing tradition in the county. There is a print of a cricket match at Canterbury in 1845 in which Beverley, one of the main Canterbury clubs, is engaged. It looks as if it is being played in the modern area of St Stephen's, with the gleaming white Hales Place, since destroyed, in the background, the modern Beverley pub nearby. There are photographs of nineteenth century county matches. White tents surround the playing area, just as they do today on all the county's grounds, but instead of the cars open carriages are drawn up at grassy vantage points, inhabited by ladies with wide brimmed hats, long white dresses, and white parasols. Cricket comes out of the country house world, and the sides - even as late as the nineteen fifties - were made up of the young gentlemen and the pros, who were treated as the squires treated their gardeners, as skilled men worthy of the greatest respect, so long as they kept their place.

There stand the Victorian great, top-hatted, statuesque, leaning on their bats. The round arm bowler, Arthur Mynn, with his buttocks like chopping blocks, is etched in permanent action. The great Fuller Pilch, barrel chested, stares down on us. His pads are in the pavilion, and are little more than shin pads. There is an extraordinary Rowlandson-type print of a bizarre match, sponsored by the Noblemen of Hampshire and Surrey in the year 1811 and played for a handsome purse, between two sides of apparently topless women on the Goodwin sands at low tide. There are village games in progress on noblemen's estates. There are the cigarette cards of the years between the wars, scorecards of memorable matches, and the scoreboard of the Kent total against Essex in the nineteen thirties - 803 for 4 declared, Frank Woolley 172, Bill Ashdown 332, Leslie Ames 202 not out. One hundred and fifty years of Kent cricket - of Kentish life - are to be seen in that little Gallery.

After tea Kent went easily to victory in the cold air, Graham Johnson showing the way with an innings straight out of the county's past, high backlifted and graceful, a right handed Woolley of the modern game. He was helped by the Pakistani, Asif Iqbal, who seemed determined to get on with the game or get out - perhaps because either way he would hurry the hot bath for which, poor man, he must have been longing. To think that only a few weeks back he was playing Test cricket on his own baked pitches. Round the pavilion bar, they were scenting victory. The photographs and portraits in the pavilion are from an earlier period. By the door an aristocratic haughty batsman stands, bat upraised, with high wing collar, blue bowtie, and a white panama hat with a blue band. In a glass case there is a set of razors presented to Fuller Pilch by the people of Sheffield along with his silver snuffbox. The lords, the young public schoolboys with their innocent but commanding faces, the free men of Kent, the head-gardener professionals - all gazing down on the modern medley of men and women, boys and girls, black as well as white, who crowded the pavilion, waiting for the winning hit. Asif pulled a six to long leg. Shepherd the West Indian, sent in to finish the game off struck a few hefty blows, and the highly professional multi-racial Kentish side, captained by the Scotsman Mike Denness, had recorded their third victory in a row. So to the slow saunter across the ground to the car and warmth. On the players' balcony the Kentish side was relaxing, waving to friends in the crowd below. Not a particularly distinguished match on a quite unusually vicious day, more suited to high January than May. But, along with five thousand others, I returned home happy.

3

A DAY on the
FAVERSHAM MARSHES

I FIRST HEARD about Graveney, when its Viking ship was found. About twenty-five years ago a tractor driver was working for the Water Board on the marshes near the little village when suddenly he felt his wheels jar. He stopped his tractor, and climbed down to investigate. There, under the dark brown earth, lay some wooden struts, which resembled the ribs of a ship. He had the good sense to tell his boss what he had found. His boss telephoned the Royal Museum in Canterbury, and soon archaeologists of all shapes and sizes began to descend on the field, where the ribs were exposed. It did not take them very long to announce that the remains were those of a Viking merchant ship, which had been beached around the year 800 and had never been relaunched. Soon the ship's remains were removed to the British Museum, where they are now prominently displayed.

I drove out to Graveney with an amateur archaeologist friend shortly after the discovery of the ship had been announced. I peered dutifully at what I could see of the wooden struts, when the small crowd surrounding them could be persuaded to part. But I could not muster enough enthusiasm to stay there long. It was certainly satisfying to see the evidence before my eyes of the claims made by the Norwegian organisers of 'The Viking Exhibition' which I had just been visiting in London. They had been at pains to point out that only some of their forefathers were the savage raiders of popular imagination, who drove onto the beaches riding on the sea's white

86

horses, swords held aloft, shields slung over their longboat's sides. Many were peaceful traders who landed in cargo ships. Here clearly was just such a ship. But I have never been able to reconstruct completed outlines from remains of any sort, and I soon left my friend to enjoy the conversation of his fellow archaeologists, and wandered off to have a look at Graveney's Parish Church.

My visit to the church stayed in my mind, and several years later I decided to revisit it. So I turned right off the A2, shortly before I came to the outskirts of Faversham, and made for Graveney on a windy November day. Gusts tugged at the leaves in the gutters, yellow, brown and red. They hoola-hooped before me as I drove past the snug retirement bungalows of Windermere Road and Buttermere Avenue and came to the village. I passed a converted oast house, followed by a group of council houses, and came to the Victorian village school. In the playground there was a huge orange elephant made of plastic. His long trunk formed a perfect slide for the children. Past it rose All Saints, Graveney.

I had forgotten how light the church is. As so often with Kentish churches, there is hardly any stained glass, so the church seems to be moored in the sky. The light wood of the box pews adds to the effect, while the excellent modern heating system contributed to the general feeling of good cheer. It's unusual to find oneself in a church which appears to be entirely unrestored. So I spent some time just enjoying All Saint's before I had another look at Judge Martyn, for it was the memory of the Judge, just as much as that of All Saints, which had led me to revisit the church.

I rolled back the rug and exposed his brass. There he lay, just as I remembered him, wearing the robes of a Justice of Common Pleas. His hands are piously joined together on his breast, while the tips of his fingers hold a heart on which is inscribed IHU MCY -Jesu mercy. His feet rest on a lion while a little lap dog nestles under his wife Anne's skirts. She lies beside him, a long mantle over her kirtle, wearing a horned head dress. At their feet lies the inscription. Translation from the Latin reads:

Bend down thine eyes, behold me stretched beneath this marble stone, O man my mortal fate foreshows the likeness of thine own. Look onward sadly, standing here I pray thee have in mind, How the most high and honoured life untimely death shall find. First was I judge in royal hall, now tremblingly I plead, Before my judge's bar, for doom myself assigned indeed. Comes swiftly on the day wherein my law, my praise my fame, Lose their renown, a lifeless voice scarce calling forth my name. I am not what I was of late, my corpse beneath this stone, Yet in the end in the Heaven's own light endowed, my flesh restored. I trust O God to see thy face, to hail thee as my Lord.

Judge Martyn's brass memorial in Graveney Church

How our forefathers loved these heavy reminders of death, as if death was not always around them in every house and street, in a manner which is almost inconceivable today!

The Judge recalls Archbishop Chichele in the North Choir Aisle of Canterbury Cathedral, a contemporary of Martyn's. The Archbishop lies in full regalia on a tomb chest, gazing up at the canopy above him, fringed with angels. The piers which support the canopy are covered with niches for small statues of saints. And beneath the tomb lies the Archbishop's skeleton, the bones sticking out like the ribs of the Graveney Viking Ship.

Others again - the practice was particularly popular in this same fifteenth century - favoured a memento mori. This was a real skull, which stood on a writing desk, or other daily used piece of furniture, to remind the owner of his end, which could come at any moment, and in all certainty would not be long in coming.

Shakespeare's lines, which never fail to bring tears to my eyes when I read them, repeat the theme at the end of the next century:

'Golden lads and girls all must
Like chimney sweepers come to dust.'

It was time to go.

I decided to have a late lunch in Faversham. Black clouds scudded in from the Swale. The day was rapidly deteriorating. Sheep were grazing on the dun-coloured grasses, their faces black and staring. Above them pylons strode to the sea.

Later I decided to pay another visit to Faversham's strangely named parish church, St. Mary of Charity. By the time I had found my way to the church past the great bulk of the town's brewery it was beginning to grow dark. Little particles of rain like grit stung my face, and I was glad to take shelter in the church.

I had been intrigued by St. Mary's on an earlier visit in the summer. It is one of the largest churches in Kent, and is in fact two churches, built in completely different styles. The entrance led me into the nave, which was deep in gloom, now that what there was of natural light had all but faded. To make matters worse I couldn't find the main light switches and had to rely on a very few lights spaced

89

intermittently around the large church. But as my eyes grew accustomed to the dusk, I began to see clearly the outline of the great eighteenth century nave which had so impressed me in the summer.

The nave replaced a Norman building, and displays a completely different attitude to man's life and faith. Its effect is classical, rational, optimistic. Slim, grey pillars point to a blue and white frieze of fruit and flowers above them. If the sun shines the nave is flooded with light, for there is little stained glass to hold it back. (Kent's churches, once again.)

In the summer I had found it easy to imagine the well-to-do and rather smug burghers of Faversham on a Sunday morning, two hundred or more years ago, bawling forth Joseph Addison's hymn:

> 'The spacious firmament on high
> With all the blue ethereal sky
> And spangled heavens, a shining frame
> Their great Originals proclaim.'

Many of them, as they sang, must have felt there were no problems remaining which could not be solved by clear thought and determined application. There were a few beggars who would pester them as they left Church, but they had brought their fate upon themselves. The cruel religious wars of the last century were in the distant past, along with the destruction of images and stained glass. They would make sure that such 'enthusiasm' would not recur in their lifetime. And if, like men and women from earliest times, they sought to understand the meaning of life, now at last they could know the answers.

For God had created the universe along clear, rational and beautiful lines, which reflected His mind. And God had given men reason with which they could discover His laws, and thus understand His mind. The congregation would no doubt have increased the volume of their singing when they reached Addison's last verse and praised the passage of the stars:

St Mary of Charity's Church, Faversham, showing the mixture of styles.

What though in solemn silence all
Move round the dark terrestrial ball;
What though real voice nor sound
Amid their radiant orbs be found;
In reason's ear they all rejoice,
And utter forth a glorious voice,
For ever singing as they shine,
'The hand that made us is divine'
What was it their poet Alexander Pope had written:
'God said let Newton be and there was light'?
There was no more to be said about life's meaning.

But the November dusk, with the wind surging around the church and wildly buffeting the trees on the church path, did not create such confidence. And when I made my way to the middle of the church, under the tower, the whole atmosphere changed. I peered into the chancel, and could just see the High Altar beyond. The transepts formed a church of its own - a huge twin-aisled hall church, with great hammer beam roof timbers, fading into the dark above. I was back in the thirteenth century, when this part of St Mary's was built. Where I stood was mystery and awe and fear. Here the world of the church merged with the world of the Faversham marshes outside, where dark clouds marched inland from the Swale, and reeds thrashed wildly in the wind.

The church in whose heart I now was standing had itself been rebuilt from an earlier Norman one. This had been destroyed by the townspeople - yes, destroyed, which shows the violence of the fighting - when the Abbot of St Augustine's, Canterbury, who had the power of patronage, had sacked a popular Vicar. This was a world in which people took easily to violence, a world close to that of Jesus Himself, the figure of whose twisted, tortured body on the cross could just be glimpsed on the high altar. The world of Nazi Germany, Bosnia, Rwanda, or Zaire.

So there it was before me in the half light - the Christian faith. Head or Heart? Reason or Awe? With the gale blowing from the marshes and tearing at the church roof it was no contest.

In the Navy I had experienced a number of storms at sea. They had been crashing, numbing experiences. They made many people pray who had rarely prayed before. And they prayed not because their reason had persuaded them that God existed, but because they suddenly realised that, for all the technology which surrounded them, they were very vulnerable. They prayed because they were terrified. They prayed because they suddenly realised something of the reality of life. They were back in the world of the Abbot of St. Augustine's and the furious people of Faversham.

Standing under St Mary's Tower in the dusk I remembered those war-time Sunday Church parades at sea. The sight and sound of hundreds of ostensibly non-believing sailors, gathered together on the rolling, bucking flat top of an aircraft carrier, singing 'Eternal Father strong to save' was enough to make even a cynical old Chief Petty Officer's eyes moisten.

> 'O Holy Spirit, who didst brood,
> Upon the waters dark and rude,
> And bid their angry tumult cease,
> And give, for wild confusion, peace:
> O hear us when we cry to thee
> For those in peril on the sea.'

we sang - and the words went straight to our hearts in a way which Addison's appeal to Reason could not. Once again it was time to go.

I ended the afternoon by walking along the Creek. I parked my car by the ship-building yards. The square deep red sails of the barges tied up alongside the Creek caught the rays of the setting sun. It was the lowest of low tides. The Swale was a trickle at the bottom of mud slopes which were as sticky as putty.

Along the horizon there was a bar of bright light. Ducks flew fast along it, ideal targets for local sportsmen, the reports of whose guns punctuated the silence. They startled great untidy swarms of starlings, who wheeled into the twilit sky. I had now passed the furthermost limits of the town and remembered Pip in *Great Expectations* walking the Thames marshes one night of similar wind and flurried rain. I recalled the passage again:

'It was a dark night . . . as I left the enclosed lands. On the horizon there was a ribbon of clear sky beyond the dark line of the marshes. There was a melancholy wind, and the marshes were very dismal. A stranger would have found them insupportable, and even to me they were so oppressive that I hesitated, half inclined to go back.'

I felt much as Pip did for a moment until I remembered that Pip was going to a meeting which nearly brought about his death. If *he* walked on into the night, there was no reason why I shouldn't do the same.

The only people I met were two men with metal detectors returning home. After we had established each other's harmless credentials I asked them what they had picked up. Their only find of interest was a George II penny. Perhaps the coin had been dropped by a worker at the gunpowder factory for we were standing on the site of the first works. It was an explosion at these works which had shaken St Mary's Church to its foundations two miles away and brought about the rebuilding of the nave whose outlines I had dimly seen an hour or so ago. Daniel Defoe visited Faversham a few years afterwards and wrote that the blast had 'shattered the whole town, broke the windows, blew down chimneys and gable ends not a few'. During the first world war there had been a far more devastating explosion. The works now stood in the town itself. Seventy or so people were killed and many more wounded. Most Faversham families suffered from the catastrophe.

I left the metal detectors and walked back into the dark, surrounded by the mournful cries of peewits. The Creek was filling up and the moving waters shone in the dark. When I turned back the lozenge-shaped orange lights of the boatyard recalled to mind the flares the prison officers carried in *Great Expectations* when they combed the marshes for escaped prisoners. A train rattled inland, a moving glow worm in the night. Soon I was stumbling my way around bollards and tripping over coils of rope in the yard until I found my car.

By the time I reached the motorway it was blowing a full gale. Great lorries crashed past my right ear, throwing up further cascades of water on the windscreen. At one point the wipers couldn't cope, and I had to take refuge on the hard standing. The Viking ship beached all those years ago on the estuary shore, the Judge brooding on his own death, the great timbers of St. Mary's transepts looming through the gloom while the wind buffeted the roof, the explosions at the Gunpowder factories, the racing clouds as black as bruises, and now the menace of lorries on a motorway lashed by thongs of rain. The day had turned out to be far more threatening than I expected.

4

SHEPPEY and the SWALE MARSHES

T HE VERY WORD Swale seems to suit the area. The Swale Council administers a district which stretches from Faversham to Sheerness, and sensibly refuses to treat the narrow stretch of sea which separates the Isle of Sheppey from the mainland as an obstacle between the two. Much of the area is marshland, reclaimed from the sea. Kingsferry Bridge is like a great barbican leading to Sheppey, and it only appears after you have rounded the corner from Bobbing and Iwade, those lovely marshland names.

Sheppey likes to make it clear even before you reach the island that it has little time for the soft and rounded delicacies of inland Kent. Snatched from the sea and the marshes, its crumbling cliffs conceding more each year to the relentless encroacher, it grumbles to you that this is the island of sheep not men. And there indeed they were, one hot July afternoon, thousands of them, grazing the scruffy marshes which run down to the swing bridge and the railway halt. I pressed on over the bridge, turned right at the roundabout, and made for Eastchurch. There were few trees and those that I saw were leafless. The stunted bushes were seemingly dusted by cement powder, and the corn, some of it now being harvested, was short-strawed. I was glad to stop at the village and enter Eastchurch Parish Church, heavy with incense in the hot afternoon.

Monks and nuns played a large part in the early history of Sheppey. The great abbey at Minster had been founded by an Essex princess who had married the King of Kent in the seventh century and marked the Thames crossing between the two kingdoms with a convent. Much of the island was reclaimed by monks and the land turned into a great sheep run - sheepway - by their labours, which emulated those of their colleagues in Thanet or at Romney Marsh. The noble fifteenth century church of Eastchurch with its wide nave and aisles, its low wooden panelled roof, its spreading wide rood screen and its smiling stonework, had been built and served by the monks of Boxley Abbey ten miles S.W. of Sittingbourne. They had carried the boulders of mainland chalk for its foundations from Faversham creek across the Swale to Harty Point. It was to the Point that I now drove. It was a longer drive than it looked on the map along a lane which was built for farm carts and past cars whose drivers were fearful of scrapes. I drove across the broad, hedgeless, treeless Harty marshes, a small prairieland, past dykes and black staring cows, past fishermen on canvas chairs with green umbrellas shading their somnambulant forms, until I came at last to a pub where once the ferry to Faversham creek had left for the mainland. Now the mainland looked so close it seemed that you could throw a stone across the channel. I turned and encountered a squashing boy who looked at me as if I had no business to be there. I should have known better than to ask him where the church was. There is nothing that gives people more pleasure than denying the existence of places situated nearby, which people have travelled far to see. The boy was no exception. No, there was no church there. Church in Eastchurch, yes, church in Harty, no. I consulted my guidebook. 'Approach the church through the farmyard', the writer counselled 'it looks as unassuming as a barn but is full of interest.' So I bade farewell to the squasher, whose eyes scorched the back of my neck as I drove back along the narrow lane and parked my car by Sayes Court Farm. I walked through a couple of gates and held my breath sharply at the sight now spread out before me. I had not come this way in vain.

Before me, panting in the sun, stretched the North Kent coast from Faversham, through Seasalter and Whitstable, past glinting Reculver Towers to the dim line of Herne Bay pier. The pale green marshes rolled gently down to the sea, some yachts were making for Faversham creek, a speedboat cut incisively through the water, and there, next to a derelict stone house, probably once its Rectory, stood St.

Thomas' Church, Harty. It stands, invisible from the road, its churchyard divided from the marshes by barbed wire, bushless, yewtree less, protected only by six leafless trees. A few thin gravestones rise like stacked playing cards out of the cropped grass. I could hardly believe my luck when I turned the handle of the porch and found it open. The long tiled roof battened the church down so effectively from the North that there was no room for windows in the low, northern wall. The building seemed fixed in the glow of the afternoon sun.

But the wide western windows were letting in the sunlight to the little white washed nave. The roof is wooden, Kentish style, and in the South chapel there is a strikingly carved chest, depicting a joust between two medieval mounted knights. The long spears crash on their opponent's shields, the horses are checked at full gallop by the knight's confrontation, and the faces of the onlookers are as vivid as those of the combatants. The origin is in dispute. Some say that the style is Belgian or German, and that the chest was dredged up from the Swale to find peace in this marshland chapel-of-rest. And it is peace which the vicar commends to those who visit his church, a commodity rare as rubies in the modern world. Carry it away with you in your hearts, he urges us in a notice designed for casual wayfarers like me, so that it will still be there as you drive over the Kingsferry bridge to join the cars hustling and manoeuvring for position at the A2 crossing, or as you go to bed in your Leysdown chalet and try to ignore the noise of your neighbour's radio. 'Visitors will, I hope, find peace and absolute tranquillity in this place' he writes 'for the same solemn majesty of wind, rain, and sunshine lives on in Harty today as in days gone by and nature still reigns in her own right over the great marshes.' I could only say 'Amen' to that.

Time was advancing by now and I wanted to look at Minster, Sheerness, and Queenborough before night fell. I took the road up the whale back of the island to its highest point where Minster Abbey stands. It was once the centre of Sheppey though now, so remorseless is the sea's erosion, it stands only half a mile from the coast. It was the abbey's situation which attracted the Danes who spotted it from their long-ships and swooped exultantly upon it as they had done on its sister at Minster-in-Thanet, raping and killing the abbess and her nuns, looting its treasures, and burning down the great church. But another abbey had taken its place until the dissolution of the monasteries had finally done for it in Henry VIII's reign and its wealth had been grabbed by The King's Treasurer, Sir Thomas Cheyney, Lord of the manor of Sheppey. His lugubrious alabaster effigy, complete with straggly beard, lies stretched out in the parish church today.

The nuns' abbey church was merged with the parish church of Minster - the two buildings can still be mistaken for two churches - and the only survivor of the old nunnery appears to be the gate house. The great cool church with its wide chancel and aisles has other effigies to show, including another alabaster figure of a knight, who is thought to have been the Duke of Clarence, brother of Edward IV and Constable of Queenborough Castle. Condemned for high treason the poor man apparently chose as his form of execution to be drowned in a butt of malmsey wine, as strange a choice, one would have thought, as a man could make. Outside, the tombstones in the graveyard have been lifted and placed around the church wall so that there is a wide expanse of closely cut grass running up to the stone walls of the abbey, giving an ample air, all the more welcome in that rather mean little town. To the south there are fine views over the Swale which can be seen for once at one's leisure owing to the liberal provision of seats in the churchyard. (There, oh there, is an object for your charity! One hundred pounds left in your will for the provision of seats in a quiet churchyard or public garden is money very well spent.)

I regretted driving to Sheerness even before I reached it. The old naval dockyard, which was first laid out by Samuel Pepys in the seventeenth century at this crucial strategic point where the Medway runs into the Thames, is now an industrial estate, and banned to visitors. No doubt I could have gained admittance if I had tried hard enough but I was beginning to grow hungry and the slagheaps of rusted scrap iron were hardly attractive. Great pylons strode through the industrial waste land, like the fowlers of the fenland who used to stalk their prey on stilts. I drove straight to Queenborough. Queenborough High Street is as wide and noble as the High Streets of Tenterden or Cranbrook, but the condition of its houses seemed very different. There was indeed the gracious late eighteenth century Guildhall, projecting over the roadway on columns, made of yellow brick, with a centre window whose arch takes up much of the building's front. But there was little else to admire and much to deplore, peeling house fronts, cheap in-filling, a fine pair of nineteenth century houses falling into delapidation, all its windows broken and boarded up. It was rundown, sad, like so much of Sheppey. I walked to the end of the little jetty. The sun was beginning to drop down behind the Isle of Grain, sailing boats rocked at anchor, gulls squawked and lamented, and the eternal fires on the tops of the oil refinery chimneys flared away. Sheppey was not so very different from its past, after all. An agricultural wasteland has been changed into an industrial one. It is time some modern monks reclaimed the debris of the industrial estates as the monks of Minster once reclaimed the Swale marshes.

5

CHATHAM ROYAL NAVAL MEMORIAL

I HAD BEEN meaning to visit the Royal Naval War Memorial at Chatham for a long time. It was partly because the Memorial commemorates Chatham-based naval officers and men, and I was a Chatham rating during the later years of the Second World War. But it was also because the Memorial is such a magnificent sight when one glimpses it suddenly from the town below, through gaps in the houses. I wanted to have a closer look at it, and finally did so one sunny June morning.

I parked my car in the Town Hall car park and panted my way up a steep and dusty path through scruffy woods and bushes. Finally I emerged into sunlight and walked through long grass until I reached the Memorial. Below lay Chatham with its concrete blocks of supermarkets, little back-to-back houses and multi-storeyed car parks. The traffic fumed in its narrow streets. Straight ahead was high ground - Gad's Hill and Great Chattenden Wood above Frindsbury. A train was slowly snaking its way towards London. Far to the west the sunlight glinted off the bonnets of the cars as they crossed the Medway Road bridge. I decided to make a day of it. I returned to the car for my sandwiches and scrambled my way up the hill again, pausing more frequently than now perhaps my pride allows me to admit, to take a breath.

The Memorial stands on the top of the hill and is dedicated to the dead of both world wars. In its centre a tall white obelisk - it is this which you see from the town below - points to the sky, topped with a green ball. Four winged cherubs launch into the heavens from the obelisk's peak. From the top of the ball peeps a tiny apologetic cross. I only saw it because of the points of sunlight which flashed from it. Twenty yards from the obelisk a tall semi-circle of white Portland stone has been built. Bronze panels stand at the base of the obelisk listing the dead of the First World War. Similar panels have been built within the semi-circle of Portland stone, naming those killed in the Second.

The Memorial is entered through a blue iron gate. Above it are written the familiar words:
'All these were honoured in their generations and were the glory of their times.'

(I couldn't help wondering whether the words were true. Many servicemen I knew felt - particularly in the Far East - that those back home, unless they were personally involved with them, scarcely gave them a thought.)

At the side of the gate the system of commemoration is defined with typical Naval precision:-

'The names on this memorial are arranged according to year of death... Within each year they are arranged according to service (e.g. Royal Navy, or Royal Marines), within each service according to rank, and within each rank in alphabetical order according to surname.'

I chatted for a while with a painter engaged in painting the iron gates on a step ladder. We both wondered how long the Commonwealth War Graves Commission would be able to bear the cost of maintaining this and other memorials, and for how long they would be visited. Then I went inside to look more closely at the two memorials.

It was immediately obvious which war the obelisk commemorated. On it is inscribed:

'In honour of the Navy and the abiding memory of these ranks and ratings of this port who laid down their lives in defence of the Empire and have no other grave than the sea.'

Only an inscription of the nineteen twenties could talk about 'the Empire'.

The different actions listed on the obelisk and on the semi-circle commemorating the second world war reflect the difference of the fighting in which the Navy took part during the two wars. In the first war the memorial gives pride of place to what it calls *General Actions at Sea*. It lists:

Heligoland
Coronel
The Falklands
Dogger Bank
and   Jutland

The amount and intensity of these set piece naval encounters between the battleships, cruisers and destroyers of the British and German fleets turned out to be far less than either side expected. Nevertheless Jutland in particular was a battle of epic proportions, which led Churchill, the First Lord of the Admiralty at the time, to refer to the British-Commander-In-Chief, Admiral Beatty, as 'the only man who can lose the war in an afternoon'. By contrast the Second World War actions carved on the white stone of the semi-circle are almost entirely combined operations with the army and the air force. They are in defence of landings on enemy shores, or of merchant ships in convoy, such as the D-Day landings, Russian convoys, or landings on the Philippines.

The amount of single ship actions fought in the First World War surprised me. Virtually none are listed in the Second.

But it was the sheer numbers of men who were killed in the Second War which held me. It is all the more terrible when one considers that all Royal Navy men were based at one or other of three ports - Chatham, Portsmouth and Devonport. Presumably the numbers of names on each of the Second World War memorials are only roughly one-third of total naval losses during the war.

I have always thought that the numbers of those killed in the Second World War over all were far less than in the First. A glance at any village war memorial bears me out. But the numbers of names on these memorial panels are much the same for both wars. It was this that weighed me down - the sheer numbers of those who 'have no other grave than the sea'. Neither then nor now, as I write, can I properly take them in.

Some differences between the occupations of those killed in the wars were striking - some, indeed, puzzling. What, for instance, did the 50 trimmers do who were killed at sea in one year - 1914? Presumably they were sail-maker's assistants. If so it shows how much sail-making continued in the First World War navy. But whose were the sails trimmed and why? And how old were the boys - 50 of them in 1914 alone, 30, most surprisingly of all, in 1941 - when they were killed? I knew that in Cobbett's time boys of 12 or less were engaged in active service, but I never knew that boys - i.e. young men under the call-up age of 18 - still went to sea in the Second World War. Nor did I expect the difference in numbers of officers killed compared to men. Even allowing for the difference in numbers of officers and men aboard ship the figures stand out. In 1914 - and the proportion was higher in later years in both wars - 20 officers (from Admiral downwards) were killed, compared to 450 able seamen. But I kept on returning to the length, the terrible length, of the death list.

The Duffel Coated Sailor

And most of those killed were so young - even if they were over 18 most were no more than boys, or so it seems today.

It took me 2 hours or so to inspect the memorials and afterwards I sat in the midday sun to eat my sandwiches in a daze. The difference between the way in which these men died - being burnt alive, or drowned protractedly at sea, processes so quaintly described on the obelisk as 'laying down their lives' - and the gentle Kentish countryside around the Memorial made my eyes sting with tears. Above sang the larks, in the distance a persistent cuckoo sang normally, not minded to change his tune, just because it was June. The high feathery grass, interspersed with wild barley, swung in the wind. In the distance the noises of a cricket match competed with the shouts and cries from a primary school playground. And I recalled that early scene in *Great Expectations* to which I have referred before in these pieces. In it Pip, huddled close to Joe, and warm in the comfort of his tightly held hand, watches as the convict is dragged aboard his prison hulk:

'The ends of the torches were flung hissing to the water and went out, as if it was all over with him.'

After lunch I returned to the memorials for one long, last look. As I was sitting musing in the sun, an elderly man in white shirt sleeves, turned out as if on parade, stumped towards me with a stick. He was a regular Navy Chief Petty Officer Engineer, who served for 35 years. He was the first to arrive, he told me, of a little and annually dwindling group who assembled in the semi-circle of the Second World War memorial on this occasion - 52 years to the day -to remember their comrades. They had been part of the crew of 'H.M.S. Boadicea' and they had been torpedoed by a German plane shortly after D-Day. Out of a ship's company of 186 men, 12 survived. The captain had gone down with his ship, but his son - now aged 70 - regularly led the survivors and their relatives (and now their survivors) at a service to commemorate the ship's sinking. They had held such services ever since 1946.

Ten years ago they had hired a boat and dropped a wreath on top of the waters off the Isle of Wight where the remains of 'The

Boadicea', on clear days, can still be seen. He thought there would be about ten of them today. Like the painter, he too wondered how long their memorial services would continue.

After we had talked for a few minutes I shook his hand and walked quickly down the hill to my car. The cricket match was still continuing and the larks sang as merrily as ever - though the cuckoo had flown away, and the children were back in school. Life, as everyone says lightly after a calamity, goes on. But I was still thinking of those young men in the waters off the Isle of Wight, fighting for life, finally joining their ship on the sea's bottom. What was the title of that novel on my shelves whose words now returned to me with a new meaning? *The Light and the Dark*.

6

AYLESHAM: THE RISE and FALL
of a MINING COMMUNITY

Part One

I FIRST SAW Snowdown Colliery in the early nineteen fifties. We were having a family holiday at Deal. One hot summer day I was travelling by bus to Canterbury to visit the Cathedral. Sitting on the upper deck, I took in the smiling scene. On both sides of the road golden fields of wheat and barley moved lazily in the gentle breeze. Most of the hay had been harvested. The apples were growing firmer by the hour, the plums a darker red, and the damsons a darker blue. We passed an occasional cherry orchard where some of the ladders were still in place though the picking had been completed. I was on the point of nodding off, reminding myself romantically that I was riding through the Garden of England, when I saw in front of us the unmistakeable outline of a colliery winding tower, with its attendant great wheel. By it and behind stood several large slag heaps. Despite the hot sun, there were deep pools of water in the cinders and tarmac round the pit head. As the bus drew up at the bus stop opposite the pit entrance I read the large notice: 'National Coal Board. Snowdown Colliery.' Now I was wide awake.

The bus then took a detour and stopped at various points in Aylesham, the nearby village where the miners and their families lived. This was a very different world from the gentle domesticated villages through which we had been riding, with their black and white timbered cottages, pink peg-tiled roofs, and cosy pubs. The Miners' Mission Church, the Working Men's Clubs, the large mock-Georgian pub, the Coop. fronting the village green spoke the language of heavy industry. Before we came to Aylesham we passed short cloth-capped men exercising their greyhounds and whippets. Slowly it came back to me. There was a coalfield in East Kent, and its discovery had something to do with the excavations for the Channel Tunnel.

When we returned home at the end of our holiday I went to the local library to find out more about the Kent coalmines. They had indeed developed from the first diggings for the Channel Tunnel, which had revealed coal at the foot of Shakespeare Cliff at Dover. The government, on the advice of the War Office, had stopped the Channel Tunnel project in 1882, fearing that the French might invade through it. But the discovery of coal had confirmed what geologists had been saying, about the likelihood of there being a coal field in South East Kent. The coalfields in the Pas de Calais area were only thirty miles from Dover. The two regions had once been joined across the Channel by a land bridge and the geology was similar. The search for coal was on, and in 1890 the experts were proved right. Coal was found.

During the next twenty years some forty borings were made in the inverted triangle which extends from Dover at its base to Ramsgate in the north-east and Canterbury in the north-west. 'Navvies', almost all of them from outside the area, travelled from one boring to the next. In the end Tilmanstone and Snowdown collieries started production shortly before the outbreak of the first world war. Chislet colliery opened four years later.

After the war the forecasts of the amount of coal which was to be found in East Kent grew wildly optimistic. Professor Abercrombie, in a regional survey, looked forward to the opening of 18 collieries. They would provide work for a further 70,000 men. The region's population would double. In July 1921 'The Dover Express' talked about the 'transforming of the Garden of England into one vast coalfield'. In the end the only post-war colliery to be opened was at Betteshanger. It produced high quality coal, whose seams were mined under the Channel, half way to France.

At first the miners at Snowdown Colliery lived in villages round about, particularly in Nonington. They came from mining areas all over Britain. As one man put it:-

'We came from Lancashire, South Wales, Scotland, Ireland, Yorkshire and Nottinghamshire. We were like the bloody Foreign Legion.'

They brought with them, like their employers, the entrenched attitudes and the atmosphere of industrial warfare which had always characterised the mining industry. Bitter disputes between owners and men occurred at Snowdown with fierce fights between police, blacklegs and pickets. The climax came with the General Strike of 1926, and the nine months miners' strike which followed it. In the summer of 1927, when strike pay had dwindled to 1/- a week, and the end of the fruit-picking season was in sight, they were forced back to work.

The building of Aylesham Village began in 1926. It occupies a shallow valley in the North Downs, and people have lived there for thousands of years. There is evidence of Roman farmsteads and of cultivated fields around them. But its name means Aegel's settlement. Aegel was a Saxon chief whose power must have extended over a wide area round about, since the crossing of the Medway at Aylesford was named after him. His settlement must have all but died out, since no building survives, and there is no mediaeval church. By 1926 all that was left was Aylesham Wood and Farm.

The site was chosen because it was half way between Snowdown Colliery and a proposed new pit at Adisham, three miles away. Abercrombie was convinced that there was as much coal in Adisham as at Snowdown. He conceived Aylesham as the town where miners from both collieries would live, and expected it to have a population of 10,000 - 15,000. In the event it was deemed uneconomic to open a pit at Adisham, and Aylesham settled down to a village of 5000 people, whose miners worked chiefly at Snowdown. Abercrombie was determined to build a new town, far removed from the smoke-grimed streets of back-to-back houses in the old mining areas. He modelled Aylesham on Welwyn or Letchworth Garden Cities in Hertfordshire, new towns, built at the turn of the century, with the emphasis on space and on the separation between a town's industries and the homes of the workers who were employed in them. He planned detached and semi-detached houses, with small terraces of houses. The houses were to have large gardens. There were to be numerous green open spaces, four churches, seven schools, a hotel, a cinema, a technical institute, a town hall, and two hospitals. Driving round Aylesham today, you can still see that many of Abercrombie's dreams have been realised - in particular the large amount of green spaces which the villagers enjoy. But though a railway station was opened in 1928, and a brass band and male-voice choir founded the year after - quite an undertaking for a middling-sized village - his full vision remained on the architect's drawing-board. It can still be seen, in all its ambitious grandeur, reproduced in the sketch plan displayed in the middle of the village square.

But though Adisham pit never materialised Snowdown expanded after the collapse of the strike. Coal was plentiful, and the owners advertised in Midland and Northern newspapers for miners. Some men literally walked from their homes; for example 200 miners from St. Helen's, Lancashire. By national mining standards the wages in the Kent coalfields were good, though the accident rate was high. Soon there were more applicants than jobs and men were forced to return home. By 1930 the number of miners in Kent had doubled. They continued to come from all over the country.

Many of these new men came to Kent because there were no jobs for them at home. A secretary of the Kent branch of the National Union of Mineworkers later put his finger on the reason why some men, like himself, had come:-

'A lot of the men were militants from 1921 and 1926, men who were prepared to stand up and be counted. They were black-booked in the collieries and couldn't get jobs, so they came to Kent with assumed names.' That tradition of militancy was to remain to the end.

The conditions at the coal face shocked men who were accustomed to hardship and great danger in their own coalfields. 'Conditions did improve slightly in the 1930s', recalled a Welshman. 'But the heat and the water - you had to lift your shoes to drain them out.' A Yorkshireman who came to Kent in 1929 remembered the work vividly:

'The water seemed to come down faster than the Thames. In the headings it used to flood a yard deep. Where the face had dropped down, you might get four foot of coal at one end, two foot at the other. It wasn't a universal seam as you get in Yorkshire or Wales. The seams rolled about like waves.'

At the face the men wore nothing but 'a belt' and clogs. Some would take as much as eight pints of water with them on the shift. Men living this sort of life are bound to become a race apart, particularly if they are housed, as were the married men, in colliery houses, owned by the company. Not that the owners, as we have seen, built badly. On the contrary the miners' houses were very solidly built and pleasant to look at. Their walls were of red and pink brick, or cream coloured, with pink tiles, chosen no doubt, to match the peg-tiled roofs of the old villages round about. But the miners and their families felt, and were made to feel, looked down upon. Single men, if they applied for lodgings in the villages round about, or in Deal or Canterbury, complained that they were charged more just because they were miners. Or they would see 'No miners need apply'

112

at the end of an advertisement. Some shops refused to serve them, they said, and local landowners complained that the worst poachers were always miners.

When I came to live in Canterbury during the nineteen seventies I read a vivid account of mining life in East Kent written in the history of the Kent branch of the union, an account based entirely on the memories of the men themselves. I heard of the recent long drawn-out battle between pickets and police at Snowdown during the Strike of 1972-4. Ten years later, when we had moved to Adisham, I learned more about Aylesham life through the local church, which had regular contacts with St. Peter's, Aylesham. Then came the 1984 strike, which arose nationally, directly from Arthur Scargill's pledge that if the Coal Board closed Snowdown, he would bring out every miner in the country. But, although I lived nearby, I still knew very little about my neighbours' lives. It was left to the Aylesham Community Play to enlighten me.

Abandoned Snowdown Colliery today.
The winding wheel has been taken down and the slagheaps used by local bikers.

113

Part Two

The play originated, several years before its production, along the Victoria Embankment in 1987. Two coachloads of Snowdown miners and their supporters had joined the long lines of banner-carrying demonstrators protesting against the government's policy of pit closures. As they walked along the route, they began talking to a professional community play producer, John Oram. Oram had been producing plays which set out to express the lives of various communities in the country - especially in the North - for several years. He found the story the Snowdown marchers had to tell so fascinating that he determined to visit the area for himself. Here, very probably he would find just the material he needed for his next play.

He was booked for several years ahead, but he did not forget his conversations. Like me he drove through the fields and orchards of East Kent, with their snug villages 'when suddenly' as he recalled 'Aylesham appeared at the end of a green lane. I felt I had entered a town in the North of England . . . Working men's clubs and chapels and in the distance . . . Snowdown Colliery. It was typical of the image of the north, misty, wet and cold.'

He soon decided to spend as much time as he could in Aylesham. He lived in the village, sleeping, sometimes for nights on end, with local families. He listened while men, women, and children relived their experiences. He heard how families had come to Aylesham from all over the country. He learnt what it was like to work an eight-hour shift, crawling a mile to the coal-face, along a corridor whose roof scraped the skin off your back all the way. He heard about the good times of the fifties and sixties, the strikes of 1972-4 and of 1984, and finally the closure of the pit on which the village depended for its livelihood. He soon had more material than he knew what to do with, and he set to work. Two years later in the summer of 1996, 'Over and Under the Earth' opened in a large blue circus tent, pitched on the outskirts of Aylesham. It played for two weeks.

The play worked backwards in time. When the lights went up, all eyes were concentrated on the high grimy winding wheel of the pit shaft. By contrast in came the Ring Master, in dazzling red velvet tail coat and top hat. He was the master of ceremonies throughout, and was accompanied by a zany girl-clown, gangling and leggy, with ballet skirt and striped stockings, Afro hair with curling rags and a beautiful white painted face. The wheel hung from the roof and was thirty feet high. Slowly it began to collapse. As it reached the ground we saw that it was not solid, but that it was made of a faded pile of fabric. It lay in a heap on the floor of the tent. And we realised that the beginning of the play was the end of the story. 'The day the headgear came down' said a character. 'I remember it . . . No ceremony, no brass bands, no choir. No best suit, no polished shoes.'

So, almost immediately, we were back three years at the last miners' strike. We saw the Union meeting which preceded it. One lone objector demanded a strike ballot. He was swept aside by the rest of the Union members, who went for immediate action. So began the marches and speeches, monitored by police, portrayed by cardboard cut-outs with riot shields chained together. One lone 'scab' was jostled and reviled as he tried unsuccessfully to fight his way through the pickets to work. We saw the women's support groups who gave their men the support which their grandfathers had missed sixty years earlier in the General Strike. A gigantic papier mache Margaret Thatcher, beak-nosed on stilts, with a wide grinning mouth, swayed around the tent smiling, waving her handbag, proclaiming platitudes, and always dominating the scene. When she had won, and the men had returned to work, they did so defiantly chanting 'The miners united will never be defeated.' But they had been.

Now followed forty successive short turns in the middle of the circle - circus style. Many were spoken by the actors, who expressed themselves in their own words rather than following a set text, for they were speaking out of their own lives. Others were mimed or sung. So we saw the school mistress lecturing the bad boy. Girls and boys played with shrimping nets in the Adisham pond, hurling abuse at each other. We were back in the golden days of the fifties when the pit owners had gone, their place taken by a benevolent Coal Board. Strikes were unknown. Everyone knew one another, and

Scenes from 'Over and Under the Earth',
the Aylesham Community Play of 1996

almost everybody helped every body else. Holidays were guaranteed, and during some weeks in the summer the pit closed down altogether. Then the whole village went off to Margate and spent days on those golden sands. While the kids played and their mothers watched over them, their fathers lay flat out on a deck chair, newspapers flopped over their face. Costumes stayed the same from the thirties. Bisto kid children. Women with wrap-over sleeveless aprons, turbans and cardigans. Men in black waist-coats, with braces, collarless shirts and peaked caps. Only the girls in the sixties were different, with their beehive hairdos, their short full skirts, and their tight waist lines.

In between the turns a wooden cage was trundled periodically into the ring. In it sat a mother and two kids at a table. Tense and bitter she sat there night after night waiting for her husband to return from the pub. Finally she locked him out, fetched a basin of water and a cloth, wiped the kids' hands and faces, and sent them to bed.

Then the action went under the earth. A procession of men crawled through wooden picture frames. Suddenly, out of nowhere, came an explosion. Two men were trapped, one of whom soon died, screaming 'Jesus'. He was carried into the cage by two of his mates. When they brought him through the front door they took off their caps, folded them and twisted them in their hands. The miner's little girl asked: 'Is he drunk?'

The miner's wife, joined by his black-shawled mother, set to and washed the corpse. After the grim task was completed, his mates, who had stood all the time with their eyes on the floor, picked up the body, lowered it into a sheet, and carried it away.

The section on the second world war was the only one of the turns which pictured life as it might have been in many other areas of the country - not that the scene was any less vivid because of that. Chamberlain's sepulchral voice told us that 'we are now at war'. Air raid sirens wailed. Bombers like big black wasps circled the tent. But it seemed surprising that the brief strike in 1942 was not shown. Aylesham miners had downed tools as one man, when a group of them was sent to Maidstone gaol for poaching from a local landowner. All over the East Kent Coal Field the miners followed suit. Ernest Bevin,

117

the previous Secretary of the Transport and General Workers union, was Minister For Labour in Churchill's Coalition Government, and the supreme commander of the home front. When he heard the news he immediately ordered their release, so that the men served only 24 hours in prison. The celebrations of the poachers' victory in the Aylesham and Snowdown Working Men's Clubs went on long into the night, while black-out restrictions were ignored. The party would have given John Oram one of his most hilarious scenes.

Poaching formed a regular theme. While the men were drawn to poaching, the women took to calling on local farmers and begging surplus food. One wife was shown begging for a sheep's head with which to feed her family. I could only admire that woman's skill as a cook, and wonder how many women under sixty could deal with a sheep's head today - in Aylesham or anywhere else.

Other more law-abiding men spent as much time and energy as they could spare after work in their back gardens. Often, as if that didn't provide enough land, they took on an allotment as well. The Annual Show of the Village Produce Association was the scene of fierce competition. One character in the play claimed that the roots of his parsnips could be seen peeping through the coal seams below.

The villagers were proud too of their chickens, and loved to feed their families on newly-laid eggs and buy fresh milk from the local farms. But this brought danger. One much loved elderly woman, still living in the village, contracted TB as a child from the milk her parents had bought. Tiny and using a motorised wheelchair she is a living reminder of the days before pasteurisation and penicillin.

As the men who took jobs at Snowdown colliery settled their families into the village they were faced with the relentless demands of the 'tally man', demanding his Hire Purchase payments. Some of the families couldn't keep up. There was nothing for it but to do a flit. So round the circle of the big top, and under an eerie suspended man in the moon, a procession of tiptoeing families, with wheel barrows piled high with furniture, left the village. I couldn't help wondering where they would finish up. So, back to the founding of the village in 1926. As Snowdown expanded, the married men wanted to bring down their families to join them. We saw the pit overseer offering them the choice of new solidly-constructed houses, brandishing a bunch of keys at them. The men were delighted to do so. For the houses were equipped with luxuries they had never known at home - running water with inside baths and toilets and electricity.

But the streets had not yet been built. The houses stood in lanes of deep mud and churned clay. At night they stood in darkness, without street lighting. Many of the men were proud of the challenges they faced. As one proud householder put it, they were 'frontier's men and women'. But it was different with many of their wives. We saw a smart young bride who arrived from the North to join her husband. She had been put down at Adisham Station three miles away, and had walked across sodden country, carrying her suitcase. When her husband showed off their first home with pride, she tried to like it. Suddenly she could stand it no longer and fled for home.

The play ended with the huge cast - men, women and children - parading round the circle. Their theme was 'The Future' and as they danced they cried out 'Yes, Yes' to it and pointed to the roof of the great-top. They were welcoming the future and saying that despite the closure of the pit Aylesham would remain the same. For all their fervour I found myself doubting if this would be the case.

Of course, it is true that the Community Play romanticised Aylesham's story. As the Ringmaster, who held the forty turns together from beginning to end, said: 'There are no good old days really', if you look closely enough at any of them. A community is admirable, so long as you go along with its views. That scab must have suffered terribly. It is said that, twelve years after the end of the strike, some families are still ostracised. A woman behind me exclaimed, as we left: 'It wasn't fair on the police. We had a good policeman and he had a terrible time.' I heard another woman saying 'Mrs. Thatcher . . . she had to do it when all's said and done.'

But no village surely can ever have had 70 years of its history summarised so brilliantly on stage. I shall remember the evening for years to come.

119

7

ROMNEY MARSH
THE CLEARANCES of the MARSHES
and the MARSHLAND CHURCHES

SHORTLY AFTER we came to live in Canterbury, we were asked out to dinner by friends in Rye. The November night was cold and still, and the sky was speckled with snowflakes. There seemed no reason, nonetheless, to change our plan which was to drive across the Marsh to Rye along country lanes, even though we were complete strangers to the marshes. Everybody told us how the coast-line, along which the main road from Hythe to Hastings runs, was lined with bungalows, holiday chalets, and holiday camps. Opinion was unanimous. If we wanted to see the Marsh proper by day or by night we must go inland. All went smoothly, and we arrived at our friends' house on time.

We left around 11pm, by which time the snow was falling steadily, though the flakes remained small. A full moon was now riding high and we decided to return home the same way, fired by the bravado of ignorance, perhaps, or, more prosaically, by our hosts' excellent red wine. The snow stopped falling shortly after we left Rye, and the moon illuminated the crusted road like a powerful search light. While the road was straight there was little fear of skidding. It was round the many corners that I crawled the most circumspectly. There seemed to be a drainage ditch close to each corner, and we had no wish to spend the night in one. All was well, however, and we were in bed before 1am.

Fragments of the Roman port lie beneath Lympne Castle,
facing the Military Canal and the farmland of the Romney Marsh,
which was once under the sea.

It is nearly thirty years since that night but the scene remains as clearly in my mind as if I drove that way last week. The moon struck a multitude of sparks off the water in the drainage ditches and the crusted snow. The flat marshlands seemed to be putting on a great display of sparklers, so many that they distracted attention from the stars. Through them could be seen the black bulk of the farms. They lay, long and low, like sleeping cats, with their buildings forming their outstretched paws. Several of the marsh churches could be seen etched clearly against the great dome of the sky - Brenzett, Ivychurch, Newchurch, Burmarsh. We could even see the tower of distant St. Nicholas, New Romney, and the four thin pinnacles at its corners. This seemed to me to be the 'real Marsh', an introverted world apart, withdrawn from the rest of us. 'The world' says a Kentish proverb 'is divided into Europe, Asia, Africa, America, and Romney Marsh'. That night I didn't think the saying fanciful.

I'm writing loosely, as an outsider does, of Romney Marsh, as if that marsh covered all the 50,000 drained acres south and south-east of the hills from Oxney to Lympne. But in fact there are 3 areas of drained marshes, all cleared at different times. The original Romney Marsh lies south and east of those hills as far as a line drawn from Lympne to Old Romney. When the Rhee Wall was built the area east and south east of it was drained until Romney Marsh extended to the sea. Finally the marshes west of the wall as far as Oxney and south west as far as the coast from Camber to Dungeness were cleared. All that area is the Walland Marsh. It took 1300 years to clear the three marshes.

Drainage of the marshes is generally described in terms of careful banking, ditching, and draining by man - the work which caused the firework display which had so overwhelmed us that night. But in fact man and nature worked closely together. During these long centuries the sea was continually building up banks of shingle along the coast from Winchelsea to Hythe. Thus there was more land available as it encroached eastwards upon the sea. At the same time rivers and streams deposited alluvium along their banks, which had the same effect of increasing land at the expense of water. And finally, during

Another view of Roman remains at Lympne Castle

1300 years there were changes in the relative levels of land and sea, which had the same effect of creating more land.

The Romans began the long clearance of the Marshes. They established a large port at Lympne - Port Lemanus - which stood then on the Rother (Limen) estuary. Sections of their Channel fleet lay at anchor there, along with the other Roman Channel ports at Dover and Richborough. Underneath the hills where Lympne Castle now stands, the Romans built a fort of 10-11 acres in extent with 12ft thick walls standing 20ft high. When the Rother silted up, the fort and quays began slowly to crumble down the hill. Indeed many of the fort's bricks, stones and tiles, those which survived the pillage of the fort's materials by the Norman Archbishop Lanfranc to build Lympne Church on the hills above, still lie scattered over the sloping fields. The big Romney Marsh sheep, fringed and woolly, graze among the ruins of what is now called 'Stutfall Castle'. Nearby their lambs play 'I'm the King of the Castle' on the slabs of stone which once formed the quayside of the Roman port.

There seems to have been no particular reason why the Romans built a seawall at Dymchurch, which eventually extended, long after they were gone, to Old Romney, and began draining the Marsh. Only later were sheep pastured on a large scale on the drained lands, a policy developed by the monks at Christ Church, Canterbury, who became the landlords of much of the Marsh. Perhaps the Romans, like the Dutch, a thousand years later, who made a nation out of the sea, or the East Anglian landowners who drained the Fens, simply wanted to create more agricultural land, rightly believing that, once the operation was completed, it would prove fertile. But, for whatever reason, the centuries of clearance had begun.

The method of clearance, once the wall had been built, seems to have been one by which numbers of small islands in the marsh, on some of which men lived with their families, were joined up by ditching, banking and draining. This work was done first by the British marshmen who were found living in the marshes when the Romans arrived. It was said that the Romans worked them nearly to extinction. Later in the ninth century, Nennius writes, in his *Catalogue of British Wonders*:

'That the first marvel is the Lommen (Limen, i.e. Rother) marsh, for in it are 340 islands with men living on them. It is girt by 340 rocks, and in every rock is an eagle's nest, and 340 rivers flow into it; and there goes out of it into the sea but one river which is called the Lemn (Limen).'

Romney Marsh proper - from Hythe to Old Romney - rarely rises more than 12ft above sea level, apart from some old settlements, such as old Romney itself, or Snargate. The question arises how the Saxon landlords of the marshes - who were, as I have said, chiefly monastic - managed to attract any tenants. The original Marshmen were clearly not large enough in number first to drain and then to maintain the dried lands. It seems that many of the tenants came from the Weald, and were keen to leave the heavy and often poor Wealden land which they had been farming, once the first settlements had been cleared in the great forest. The newly dried out land seemed much more attractive than their own farms and they were glad to accept

Marshland tenancies even though they always carried with them obligations to maintain the dykes and drainage channels. The families probably maintained contact with the Weald, which would explain why so much excellent wood - especially oak - is found in Romney Marsh churches. Certainly none of that wood grew on the Marsh.

The general impression of marshland - that it is good only for the pasture of great flocks of sheep - is unfounded. The new settlers found much of the land very fertile. They grew hay, oats, beans, wheat and barley on the marshes. A thousand years later - during the second world war - they did the same, when the German blockade made maximum agricultural production imperative. And in recent years there has been considerable horticultural production, where once the land had been used only for sheep pasture.

Nor was agriculture the sole source of wealth on Romney Marsh, in the years before the great storm of 1287. There was a lot of fishing. Salt-panning, fuelled by cheap supplies of wood from the Weald, took place at the mouth of the Rother, while peat-beds were dug in the Walland Marsh.

By the Norman Conquest the original Romney Marsh - from Hythe to Old Romney - had been finally cleared. Sheep were pastured on a large scale though, as we have seen, the Marsh had not yet become the 'giant sheep run' which William Cobbett called it after the Napoleonic Wars. Around 1250 Romney Marsh was greatly expanded, when the monks of Christ Church, Canterbury, supervised the building of the Rhee Wall from the Isle of Oxney to Old Romney. Now Romney Marsh was drained to the east and north, and farm land extended to the sea all the way from New Romney to Hythe.

The monks of Canterbury Cathedral were not content with extending Romney Marsh to the sea. From 1250 onwards they began the clearance of Walland Marsh, to the south and west of the Rhee Wall, until the whole laborious operation was stopped by the Great Storm of 1287.

Near Dungeness, in Saxon times, a little port had grown up on the island of Lydd at the southern mouth of the Rother estuary. Salt-panning flourished there, and a Saxon church built, parts of which still

125

stand. In 774 the manor of Lydd was given to the Archbishop of Canterbury. The town became one of the two royal boroughs on the Marsh.

The other is at New Romney. Around 1000 a fort - burh - was built at Old Romney, which became one of the original Cinque Ports. In return for providing men and ships for the Navy, the Crown gave it special privileges in the form of exemptions from customs duties and the right to hold its own courts. There was a royal mint there, and at the time of Domesday Book the town boasted 156 burgesses. St. Clement's Church, Old Romney, still stands, dignified, massive, but on its own, close to the main Hythe - Folkestone road, a witness to earlier glories.

For the silting of the Rother which earlier had led to the closure of the Roman port at Lympne, continued. A new town was built a few miles further east at New Romney, the point up to which the Rother could now be navigated by sea-going ships. It had the privileges and status of Old Romney, and in addition a magnificent new Norman Church and Tower was built.

But the Rother continued to silt up. A V-shaped estuary extended from New Romney, with its southern mouth at Dungeness and Lydd, and its northern mouth at St. Mary's Bay. But pebbles, sand and mud continued to claim more and more of the estuary, until in 1287 an extraordinary catastrophe occurred. (Strangely the hurricane of 700 years later also inflicted great damage on New Romney, both town and church.) In the Great Storm of 1287 the Rother changed its course. Huge seas, whipped and churned by hurricane-force winds, hurled pebbles, stones, shingle and shells into the river's mouth, closing it completely. Unable to find its normal outlet, and confronted with flat land which could not contain it, the river swirled west until it reached the hills at Rye and found another permanent outlet at Camber. It went on to flood a wide area from Appledore to Winchelsea.

Though much of Walland Marsh was flooded and their work had now to start all over again, the monastic overseers returned to their long task after the Great Storm. The bell tower, which stands on the ground beside Brookland Church, was probably built originally to

126

cover a flood bell, which warned the inhabitants of approaching flood waters. For the Rother catastrophe was not the only natural disaster to engulf the marshmen and their families in the years from 1250 to 1350. There were many other great storms which led to widespread loss of life through flooding, and when the storms eased, diseases took their place culminating in the Black Death of 1348-9. It has been reckoned that during these years the population of Romney and Walland marshes must have halved. Inevitably land which was previously arable now reverted to sheep pasture, requiring far less labour. The marshes only became famous for their sheep from 1400 onwards, the last century of church landlordism. It was during the fifteenth century that sheep-farming became so prosperous that the monks were able to raise their tenants' rents. With them the nave of Canterbury Cathedral was rebuilt and the magnificent Bell Harry Tower constructed. When the monasteries were dissolved in the fifteen thirties the monks had already achieved their ambition, and the marshes had reached their modern form. Walland Marsh had been cleared from Appledore in the north, to Camber in the west, and Dungeness in the east.

Few men and women who could avoid doing so lived on the marshes. Those who did were a prey to 'marsh fever' and died young. There were no manor houses built on the marshes during the middle ages and few large farms. As for the 22 parish churches they were cared for - if at all - by resident curates, acting on behalf of their monastic superiors (or others). If the Rector appeared at all at his church he would do so simply to hold Sunday mass. For this he would receive a full stipend, a small part of which he would pay his curate. Rectors generally spent Saturday night at Rye, and rode out to the Marsh to take Mass. They would ride back when Mass was over. Cardinal Wolsey, among his many other benefices, was Rector of Lydd, though the borough was never honoured with a glimpse of the great man.

Erasmus, that savage critic of the Catholic Church, who was forever declaiming against the absenteeism of priests, was himself a Rector at one time of some Marshland churches. He was never known even to spend a night in Rye, but drew his stipends from his home in the Netherlands.

The twenty-two parish churches on Romney and Walland Marshes bear witness both to the wealth of the drained marsh lands, and to the ownership of much of that land by Canterbury Cathedral, Lyminge Minster, and the Archbishop of Canterbury. (Not that all Marsh churches were church foundations. Two of the best known - Dymchurch and St. Mary in the Marsh - were founded privately). The monks insisted that churches be built on the lands for whose clearance they had been responsible over centuries. Farm rents were used to finance building the Marsh churches, while their tenant farmers and labourers provided the labour to build them. They used stone from quarries near Maidstone or from as far away as Caen in Normandy. The stone was carried by sea to Lydd, or New Romney, or Hythe. After the Great Storm it was taken to Rye Harbour.

The transport of the wood for church-building from the Wealds of Kent and Sussex was laborious in the extreme. The trees - very often oak - were stripped to the trunk where they were felled. Then the carters set out with two or four horses to drag the great trunks along the narrow, winding and thickly mudded lanes which led eventually to where the marshland church was being built. By November the lanes were impassable. The trunks would have been abandoned, lying on fields fronting the lanes, for the law required the farmers concerned to provide land free for that purpose. In the spring, the carters returned to complete the journey to the church.

All Saints, Lydd - often called the 'Cathedral of the Marshes' - was the first of the Marsh churches to be built, while the last was the brick church at East Guldeford in 1505. As we have seen, parts of the old Saxon church still survive at Lydd, where the first port at the mouth of the River was built, later to be superseded in importance by the Romneys, Old and New. Superseded or not, Lydd was given royal borough status by Edward I. It celebrated its position by building a magnificent thirteenth century church, much of it in Caen stone, with seven bay arcades, supported by short circular piers with circular capitals. When you look up to the roof the soaring stone vaulting seems to lead your eyes up to the very sky above. The impression of a cathedral-size parish church constructed in the open Marsh air is further supported by the almost total lack of stained glass. There is nothing to block the light. Nor is there anything to mute the noise of the winds which, given half a chance, howl round the tower. The tower was the last part of the church to be built. Its builder, in the mid fifteenth century, was Thomas Stanley one of the senior masons at Canterbury Cathedral. At the same time his colleagues were constructing the Cathedral's 'Bell Harry' Tower, with its four pinnacles which jab the sky in the same way as do the pinnacles from Lydd Tower. For hundreds of years, observers on duty at the Tower's highest point warned of storms approaching from the Channel, or of floods inland. In 1940, they warned of German planes approaching in the Battle of Britain, one of whose pilots dropped a bomb on All Saints, destroying the sanctuary, rebuilt in the early sixties.

Similar destruction, though this time by the hurricane in 1987, was inflicted on Lydd's neighbour, St. Nicholas at New Romney. Much of the chancel and nave was destroyed that night. It has taken years of work by devoted volunteers, supported by local farmers who have provided materials free of charge, to make good the damage, and the job is not finished yet. St. Nicholas, which was begun about 1160-70, is built in the Norman style with aisles and round arched bays supported by massive pillars. The Tower which, like Lydd tower, can be seen from miles away over the surrounding flat marshes has a magnificently carved Norman west door, with carved shapes, birds and animals, reminiscent of the Norman carvings at Barfrestone or Patrixbourne churches.

Church building began early on the original Romney Marsh. By 1100 all the parish churches on the Marsh had been built. They were two-celled buildings, consisting of a nave and small chancel, with round arches, zig-zag and dog toothed carvings on the stone pillars, and a square east end. Burmarsh and Dymchurch are fine examples of this early style, though of course there were additions and extensions during later centuries. With the greater wealth and population which followed the building of the Rhee Wall, came new and more elaborate styles. At Brookland, for instance, a late twelfth century timber church was replaced in the early thirteenth century by a stone structure. The builders must have realised that the soft ground would not take the weight of a tower on top of the stone building. This explains the building of a bell-tower on the ground to the left of the church porch, which has two doors, like a stable, to keep out straying animals. The bell-tower was built in stages from the thirteenth century, and looks like 3 candle-snuffers one on top of the other. Its shingles were replaced recently, once again by courtesy of the hurricane, which scattered cedar-wood shingles all over the neighbourhood. There are six bells.

The nave of Brookland Church has arcades on either side of it, the pillars of which look dangerously skewed through the movement of the soil on which the church stands. (I am assured that all, in fact, is perfectly safe.) The floor is brick, and the Norman font made of lead. It was imported from northern France. Round its sides are two friezes. The higher one is of the signs of the zodiac. The lower shows the occupation in the countryside that month. So Leo (July) shows a lion and below it a hay maker, while Scorpio (October) shows a sort of frog; with beneath it a man treading grapes in a vat and holding up a bunch of grapes. The figures depicting the farm work of the month are particularly vivid, and speak to us across the centuries of the details of their daily work, month by month.

A few miles from Brookland, surrounded by munching sheep, and standing completely by itself, stands the Church of St. Thomas a Becket, Fairfield. The nearest building - a farmhouse called Becket's Barn - is a good four hundred yards away. From it you collect the large and magnificent key which turns the lock in the church door so easily that it is as if it is oiled weekly.

There is something very humble about the dumpy little church. Its main parishioners, the flocks of sheep, tear as much grass as they can find right up to the church door. It looks very much like a barn, with its steep sloping roof - or rather, two barns, standing end to end, one, the smaller, forming the chancel and the larger, joined directly to it, the nave. It is built on a specially constructed mound. From it, I have seen it look out upon flood water in the spring, which is threatening to rise and lap at its foundations. On another occasion, in January, I have seen it standing in the midst of crusty snow. The sheep were still there, nosing beneath the sparkling snow, staining it yellow in places, and marking it with their dainty footprints.

Apparently a timber-framed church stood on the same site in the middle ages, though it is difficult to see why, since no signs of habitation surround it. The present church, which looks brown in the distance, though lichened, is built, on nearer inspection, of red and blue bricks. The old timbers must have been completely reconstructed, with great crown posts holding up the roof. The contrast between the height of the roof and the tie beams of the chancel, which stand only 7 feet from the ground, adds to the general diminutive - almost twee - impression which St. Thomas gives. The church is just a tiny chancel, with a short nave leading up to it. Railings surround the altar on three sides, where communicants kneel to receive Communion.

The railings, eighteenth century box pews, and three-decker pulpit must have been taken from somewhere, along with the textboards of the Creed, Lord's Prayer and Ten Commandments, written in gold on a black background. Once again, the plain glass windows let in so much light that one feels as if one is standing with the sheep in the open air. Whether in addition to this light, it was necessary to paint the pews, pulpit, and railings white - twenty years ago they were the colour of their own wood - I am not so sure. Certainly the whole impression of St. Thomas', when one pushes back the heavy door, after threading one's way through the sheep, is one of light. There is, not surprisingly, no electricity. I would love to attend a Christmas service there after dark, the little church lit by candles and oil lights, throwing shadows at the gleaming windows, and up to the dark timbers of the barn-like roof.

I have chosen four of the 22 marshland churches which still stand on the Romney and Walland marshes where they were built. Two of them - New Romney and Lydd - are as big and impressive as any Cathedral. St. Augustine, Brookland, stays in the mind not only for its font and bell-tower. Starting at the altar and working west the styles range from the pointed arches of the thirteenth century to the perpendicular fifteenth century style. In the south-west corner of the south aisle a mediaeval mural has been uncovered from the plaster, showing the murder of Thomas Becket, while near the door stands a form of sentry-box, which serves a practical purpose which I have come across nowhere else. The parson stood in it by the graveside during funerals. He was able to concentrate on the service while the sentry-box kept the marsh rain off his best wig. St. Thomas, Fairfield, is a church on its own. When one sees it for the first time one exclaims at the sight, and its novelty never dims, however often one visits it.

Of the other 18 all one can say is 'go and look at them, perhaps two at a time, without a feeling of hurry or stress'. I would like to mention, in conclusion, only one more. That is St. Mary-in-the-Marsh, which stands deep in the marsh, with a pub, a farm, and a few houses around it. The Early English church is largely unrestored and beautifully kept. The Victorians kept away from it, to its great gain. Inside the church there is a plaque in memory of Edith Nesbit, the children's writer, who died nearby. Her husband, a handyman, built a simple wooden memorial to his wife in the churchyard when she died in 1924. The lettering on it is now difficult to decipher and at some point soon a decision will have to be made about its conservation. Perhaps this is a job which the E. Nesbit Society might like to look at.

Bibliography

F.W. Jessup   *Kent History Illustrated*

Articles in *Archaeologica Cantiana* No.107 on 'The Development of Romney Marsh' by K.P. Whitney, page 44, and 'Church Building on Romney Marsh' by Tim Tatton-Brown, page 253

Entries in Nikolaus Pevsner's *Buildings of England* - 'West Kent and the Weald' by John Newman - under individual Marsh Churches.

The Guide to St. Augustine, Brookland, by the late Anne Roper.

8

ROMNEY MARSH and WAR

A S A NATION we are strangely lax about removing ugly defence works thrown up in a hurry during wars which have long since ended. Pill boxes and concrete dragons' teeth still stand, for instance, all along the south and east coasts of England, erected well over fifty years ago against threatened German invasion in 1940. Some of the pill boxes do service as sheep pens, but most of these defence works are only of historical interest. The defence works built hurriedly along the Romney Marsh coast line to meet the threat of invasion from France in 1805 still stand where their builders erected them. Some of the Martello Towers have been converted to private homes, while the rest, though gently crumbling, stand unnecessary guard over the shingle. And the Royal Military Canal from Rye to Hythe attracts thousands of canoeists, oarsmen, walkers and campers each year.

By 1803 Napoleon controlled Western Europe from Holland to Brest. Though he had hoped that his blockade would force the British - that 'nation of shopkeepers', as he called them, borrowing a phrase from Adam Smith - to surrender, it was now obvious that it would do no such thing. There was only one answer to the 'problem of England'. She must be invaded.

Whether or not the hundred thousand men and fifteen hundred flat-bottomed barges which Napoleon had collected at Boulogne would in fact have made for the Marsh coastline, if they had been given the order to sail, or whether they would have tried to land elsewhere, nobody knows. Probably Napoleon himself had not made up his mind. When reviewing his invasion fleet in 1805 he was reported as 'uttering some energetic expressions indicative of his vexation'. In any case, the British Government regarded the Marshes as the most likely landing place. Once they had reached that conclusion, they acted with remarkable speed and decisiveness.

At first the solution seemed to be adopt the traditional Dutch answer to threatened invasion - flood the Marsh, by letting in the sea. This was rejected on financial grounds. The farmers would need more compensation money that any British government could pay. So the government, who were quick to concentrate numbers of troops at Shorncliffe Barracks, near Folkestone, which could be moved into the Marsh if invasion seemed imminent, turned to the building of coastal defences.

British generals had been impressed by an engagement with French troops in Corsica, ten years earlier, when the British had set out to invade the island. A Tower at Mortella Point on the island, manned by only thirty-eight men armed with one 6-inch and two 18-pound guns, successfully held off two British warships. It was only finally taken by land, and that after two days fighting. Sir John Moore, the General in charge of the national defences from his headquarters at Hythe, had been present at Mortella Point, and had not forgotten the round tower with a flat roof, on which stood swivel guns. He ordered that 103 of them be built in a chain from Aldeburgh in Suffolk to Seaford, Sussex. Martellos - their second letter had been changed from o to a during their change of nationality - were built from Hythe to Winchelsea as part of the Marshland's defences.

While Moore was building towers, Napoleon, was offering hostages to fortune on a gigantic scale. He ordered that a special medal be struck and issued to his soldiers, waiting to invade England at Boulogne. It was to be inscribed:-

'Descente en Angleterre. Frappé a Londres, 1804.'

This was duly administered to his men on his birthday, August 15, 1804. But he still delayed the signal to set sail.

On the other side of the Channel, thousands of navvies were building the Royal Military Canal, to run from Hythe to Rye.

At first sight, it is difficult to grasp the strategic thinking which lay behind the construction of the Canal. Only at one point - near Hythe - does the Canal run close to the shore. At its furthest point - from Appledore to Dungeness - the distance exceeds ten miles. It could never have prevented landings from invasion barges. Indeed the idea that any Canal could have prevented the French from establishing a beach-head was too absurd to contemplate for anyone with knowledge of previous French campaigns in Western Europe. As William Cobbett put it scornfully, writing after the war:-

'Here is a canal . . . made . . . to keep out . . . those armies who had so often crossed the Rhine and the Danube . . . a canal made by Pitt, thirty feet wide at the most.' (Cobbett - *Rural Rides* Vol.2 1823)

(He was wrong actually. It was seventy feet across, but his point is not effected by his underestimate.)

Yet Cobbett merely advertised his ignorance by his scorn. Moore and his engineer Colonel John Brown - a solidly English name for a Scotsman - were not thinking of trying to halt a landing. They had two clear reasons for spending £234,000 on building the Military Canal, which was not finished until 1808, long after Napoleon's men had left Boulogne and moved instead on eastern Europe.

The first was to enable troops to be moved quickly to any point on the Marsh, once it was clear exactly where the French were landing. The roads across the Marsh, which were little better than farm tracks in dry weather and which, when it rained, became indistinguishable from the surrounding wet lands, were quite unsuitable for the rapid movement of troops. They could, however, be quickly and efficiently moved by canal barge.

Brown's second objective was to seal off the Marsh, at least temporarily, from the rest of Southern England. Though probably nothing would stop the French from landing, the Canal - behind which lay the cliffs from Lympne westwards - would confine them to the flat lands south and east of it. When troops from further inland - those camped on Barham Downs, for instance - had been marched to join the forces already carried along the Canal from Shorncliffe and Hythe, the invaders could be driven back into the sea.

In 1940 the invaders, now the Germans, also planned to seal off the Marsh. Their invasion plan, known as 'Operation Sea Lion', proposed the landing of nine divisions in the first wave. Four divisions - some 26,800 men - were to be landed between Folkestone and Hastings, the great majority of the men on the shores of Romney Marsh. Two more divisions were to land between Bexhill and Eastbourne, and three between Beachy Head and Brighton. As with the allied invasions of Normandy four years later, paratroopers were to play a vital part in the plan, by dropping well behind the landing beaches along the main road from Canterbury to Folkestone. The bridgeheads were to be enlarged as quickly as possible inland to a line drawn from Canterbury to Ashford, Ashford to Tenterden, and Tenterden to Etchingham in East Sussex. By the end of Day One the Germans expected to have reached, after breaking through the defences from Hythe to Dymchurch, as far as the line Paddlesworth - Postling - Sellindge. The British were not expected to counter-attack until the morning of the fifth day after the invasion. The Germans would have had ample opportunity to build up a substantial force by then, always assuming they controlled the sea and, above all, the air above their beach-head.

British defences were not as amateur and inadequate as the millions of today's admirers of 'Dad's Army' have been led to expect. Talk of flooding Romney Marsh had been again rejected, as in 1803 (though Pett Level, west of Rye, was flooded), and the army constructed slit trenches along the seawall. The Martello Towers were manned with machine guns, while the sand and shingle were heavily mined. Inland pill boxes and Dragon's teeth were built at as many strategic points as possible, especially along the Canal. All over the Marsh, to the irritation of local farmers, obstacles to prevent the landing of gliders were rapidly thrown up - particularly groups of hop-poles, readily available for next month's hop-picking. It is by no means certain that the Germans would have landed and advanced inland as smoothly as both German and British staff-officers appear to have expected.

German headquarters, in France and the Low Countries, earlier in the year, had depended on a detailed flow of information from agents well behind the front-line. By the beginning of September, with landings due on the South coast to begin within three weeks, no such information was available about defences in the proposed landing zones. There were no spies sending back reports. On September 2 German Intelligence at last met the demands of the German High Command. Four German agents, embarked at Le Touquet in a fishing boat, were escorted across channel by two minesweepers and landed in the early hours of September 3. They landed in pairs - one at Hythe and the other at Dungeness.

The men at Hythe had been captured by sentries of the Somerset Light Infantry by 5.30 a.m. They were two Dutchmen, who had been blackmailed by the Germans for crimes known to them. They spoke hardly any English. One of them looked Asiatic (he had in fact a Japanese mother). It was his appearance together with the fact that he had shoes and binoculars slung round his neck that led a sentry to challenge him. The Dutchmen offered no resistance.

The pair who landed at Dungeness were captured separately. One of them was Dutch, and spoke excellent English. He was, however, desperately thirsty. (It seems that the spies, together with the fishermen, had been drinking heavily as they crossed the Channel.) He tried to buy cider at a pub in Lydd, and was soon arrested. His colleague, a German, survived till the next day and sent some short messages. (He had rigged up an aerial in a tree.) All four were tried in secret in November. One of the Dutchmen, for some reason, was acquitted. The other three were hanged in Pentonville the next month.

If the invasion never materialised, the war in the air, which the Germans knew they had to win if a landing was ever to occur, was fiercely fought above the skies of Kent and Sussex from mid-August onwards. Nowhere was it fought more fiercely than in Marshland skies. The machine-guns on the Martello Towers were in continual use against hundreds of low flying German bombers. Many British and German 'planes were shot down. Some of the German pilots were surrounded, after they had parachuted to ground, and threatened with lynching. One asked to be taken to German Head Quarters, assuming that the Marsh was already in German hands. Aerial fighting did not end when Hitler abandoned his invasion plans, and turned first to all-out bombing of London and other British towns, and later to the attack on the Soviet Union. The Luftwaffe Pilot whose body was discovered at Burmarsh in 1973 in his uniform, his identity disc still round his neck, had been shot down in October 1940, a month after the Battle of Britain officially ended. Only gradually, first as German concentration moved east, and then, after the allied landing in Normandy in 1944, as aerial fighting was conducted over European skies, did Romney Marsh return to peace.

Once the Germans had invaded the Soviet Union in June 1941, fights over the marshes between the Luftwaffe and the R.A.F., were less common, though they still continued. After the allied landing in Normandy on 4 June 1944 and the subsequent liberation of North France and Belgium it ended altogether. The rockets (V Ones) and Flying Bombs or 'Doodlebugs' (V Twos) which were launched across Kent by the Germans from the mid-summer of 1944 onwards were aimed at London. The marshes were left alone.

Bibliography

Romney Marsh and the Royal Military Canal by Fay Godwin and Richard Ingrams. (1980) The book contains some stunning photographs taken by Fay Godwin.

Invasion 1940 by Peter Fleming. (1957) The account of the landing of the ill-fated spies in September 1940, and of their rapid capture, is to be found on pages 185-6.

9

DODE CHURCH

I DETERMINED to visit Dode Church when I read an article about it in *The Times* in early April, 1996. (So, apparently, did about two thousand other people over Easter, which followed shortly after the article's publication.)

The story was certainly remarkable. It seemed that the Black Death of 1348 destroyed the great majority of the little church's parishioners. (Did they all die or did many of them, after the first deaths, pack their bags and move down the hill to nearby Luddesdowne?) In 1367 the Bishop of Rochester wrote to Dode's priest and told him to close the church, since there was no longer a congregation to support it. (A copy of the letter still exists.) For over seven hundred years the church slowly disintegrated until it was restored from a state of near ruin at the beginning of the twentieth century by a former mayor of Gravesend, Mr Arnold. A picture of the state in which he found it is to be seen in the church.

Dode stands in deep countryside on the North Downs half way between Gravesend and Rochester. It was built about 1100. It served only a tiny area, but qualified as a separate parish in the records of the diocese. After it had been abandoned it remained untouched until its reconstruction.

It is necessary to put this, to my knowledge, unprecedented situation in more detail. Dode, a simple early Norman church of nave and chancel, has not been altered since it was built. The windows are mere round - arched slits, one for each wall. There is no Gothic influence - whether Early English, Decorated or Perpendicular - to be seen. The roof has never been raised, the walls have never been white washed, the floor never relaid. The changes of the Reformation never touched Dode. It is as close now to its original state as a church of that date could be.

Perhaps the point is better made more positively. The walls, two feet, ten inches thick, remain roughly coursed of flint rubble. The floor remains earthen - there are no foundations - though it has recently been covered with a layer of concrete. When in use it would have been covered with straw. In the chancel the aumbry is still in place, a small cupboard for storing Communion bread and wine, holy oils, and relics (if there were any). The church is still lit by candles and wall torches. There is still no heating. The church must be frighteningly cold in winter, even if the massed candles and wall

torches, together with the heat from bodies packed tightly together, would have provided increasing warmth as the two-hour mediaeval mass developed. Though, for the sake of convenience, some moveable roughly hewn boards have been provided recently as seats, it is easy to see that most of the congregation would have stood or knelt during the services.

The church is built on a man-made mound. From it you look across the tiny valley, with green fields rising towards a gentle range of downland. There is speculation that the mound was used for Celtic worship well before the Roman occupation. Recent archaeological evidence has confirmed Roman presence on the mound. The site, in short, had been used for a variety of religious rituals for at least a thousand years before Dode Church was built.

The reconstruction at the beginning of our century was most carefully carried out. The only basic addition was the roof. The thatch, of course, had long since gone and Mr Arnold built the present roof of tiles and stone.

The church was never deconsecrated and during the nineteen fifties the Roman Catholic authorities decided to rededicate it. They called it 'Our Lady of the Meadows' and held occasional services there - the first to be held since the Black Death. But they could not protect the church from continual vandalism. Four years ago they put it up to auction, expecting that it would be bought for conversion to a private house. Instead it was bought by Mr. Douglas Chapman for £67,000, who decided to return it, in so far as he could, to its original early Norman state. The village, named after a ninth century Saxon settler, had long since ceased to exist but he called the church Dode after it.

Mr Chapman says of himself:

'I am not a churchgoer. I'm not religious, I believe in a God but I'm not a fully paid up member of any church.' His position, in short, is that of the great majority of his fellow citizens. He does not know why he bought Dode. He only knows that when he walked into the building for the auction he turned to his wife and said he had to buy it.

'I just fell in love with it' he says. 'It's a beautiful place. I decided it would be a lovely thing to look after.'

But although Mr Chapman is 'non-religious' he was determined that Dode should be rebuilt as a place of worship, what he calls 'a holy place'. After all, is it not surrounded and sheltered by Holly Hill, which is a corruption of holy hill?

'You have to go to the church itself to understand why I bought it' he says. 'You walk in the door and either say 'I understand why you bought it' or you don't. If you understand it, you are on my wavelength. I certainly didn't want to see it turned into a house . . . This is my own little campaign. I love the building, the atmosphere.'

But who will use it, and who will conduct services within its rough flint walls? The first job which faced Mr. Chapman has been partially achieved, though much, much remains to be done. You can see now what the church was like when the last priest closed the door for good, as he thought, in 1367. (The priest lived in the church, sleeping in the Rood Loft, above the great cross, which would have hung from the roof, and separated chancel from nave. Amazingly Mr Chapman has found the oak beam which the priest pulled across the church door last thing at night when he locked himself in.)

And this is where Mr Chapman's 'non-religion' comes in. He has formed a trust for Dode's administration but he remains the owner and is quite clear about the lines along which Dode will be conducted. He will work to make sure that anyone can use the church for meditation, reflection and private prayer. Any service can be held in the church, by arrangement with himself, and at times that do not conflict with local parish churches. The church will be basically Christian, but multi-faith worship can also be held there.

His ideas are clearly proving popular. When I visited Dode in early May 1996 with a group there was a list of services up till the end of July, displayed at the door. The Anglican evening service of Compline would be held twice. There was a service of Holy Communion on one evening. Three Roman Catholic priests - one described as Liberal - were celebrating mass on different days, and one threw in a picnic with it. The Metropolitan of the British Orthodox Church was celebrating the raising of incense to mark the birthday of St John the Baptist on the evening of June 24. The service was described as a simple service of intercession, scripture reading, and Biblical preaching lasting an hour. The church was open for private prayer and meditation on certain evenings. Most intriguing of all, multi-faith chanting was billed on three evenings. The services would last three hours, and the chants would be Christian, Native American, Asian Indian and Pagan Devotional.

The restoration of the interior had reached a half way stage. Mr. Chapman and his team aim to restore it entirely to its original state - when they know exactly what that was - but in the meantime temporary arrangements had been installed. The two big wagon wheels which hung as chandeliers from the roof and on which a circle of sturdy candles had been placed looked modern, with their iron suspension chains. (The candles on the sloping window sills looked far more convincing). The sheaves of corn and berries which covered the floor were only spoilt in places by what appeared to be a few plastic flowers. There were a few rather improbable wall hangings, including a splendid tall red Chinese dragon on a white background, which Mr. Chapman has hung temporarily to please some Chinese friends. There were a couple of ornate iron torch brackets on the central arch which separates the chancel from the nave which didn't look early Norman. But these will surely change as Mr Chapman achieves his final target - to restore Dode to its original state in every particular.

As I stood by the door and looked back at the interior of the little church I tried to picture the scene as it would have looked one summer Sunday Mass, seven hundred years ago, before the Black Death. The priest, flanked by two altar boys, stood at the altar. The air was hazy with incense from the priest's swinging censer - if the church could have afforded it. Round the wall sat the weakest, seated on a stone seat, the old people alongside some mothers, discreetly suckling their babies. Everyone else stood, young children clutching their parents' knees. The smells of the hayfield below the church mingled with the incense. The chanting of the Latin Mass by the

Dode Church interior

priest, punctuated by the responses of the congregation, mingled with bird song and the general sounds of high summer. A swallow suddenly swung through the door and circled the church above the heads of the congregation. Some bats hung upside down from the rafters.

And I thought how little I really knew about this little group of our ancestors, even though I have been reading history, studying history, and teaching it with an interest that seems to increase rather than dwindle for well over fifty years. I knew some basic facts about them. I knew that around 98% of them were serfs, tied to the Lord of the Manor at Luddesdowne by an arrangement that was very close to slavery. I knew that if they lived past forty they were lucky, and that their families would rarely exceed more than two surviving children. (For those two survivors their mothers would have endured six or seven miscarriages, or infant deaths.) The boys would have gone to work in the fields as soon as they could walk and continue working till they could do so no longer. Hardly any of them could read or write. They would have lived in one-or-two-roomed thatched huts, built, like the church, directly on to earthen floors. There would have been no room for any other adults, such as grandparents, if they were still alive.

I knew that the priest would probably himself have come from a family in the village. Though he would have been picked out by one of his predecessors as a bright lad and taught his letters he would probably only know the meaning of a smattering of the Latin words he spoke in the Mass. If he gave a sermon at all, it would be very simple and would chiefly consist of notices concerning parish activities. I knew that few of his flock would ever have travelled as far as Rochester or Gravesend and would rely on travelling pedlars for news of the outside world. Of wars with France, threats of invasion, or the conflict between King and barons that led to the signing of Magna Carta they would have known nothing. They were born in Dode, lived and worked in Dode, and were buried, with no memorial, in Dode churchyard. In short, I knew the curriculum vitae of the parish - and CVs are of only limited interest.

What did I really know about them? Did they believe they were eating Christ's body when they came to communicate, and if so what did that mean to them? Did they just assume that their ownership of strips of land in the three great open fields of the village was the only way they could ever own land and that this was the only method of farming known to man? Did they think that the Lord of the Manor and his lady were different sorts of people from themselves? What did they know of the Bible, which was available only in Latin, and that to the priest, who told his people as much of its story and teaching as he saw fit - or, more probably, as he knew himself? Did they believe that the terrible physical tortures of hell which were so graphically portrayed in the murals on the walls around them really awaited them, and that for eternity, if they committed wrong? What did they expect, come to that, to find in heaven if they finally arrived there via purgatory? Did they believe that such - to our eyes - terrible losses of life in childbirth were inevitable, part of God's will, or might man's intelligence in time end them? Perhaps if you believed you would soon be meeting your loved ones in the next world - really believed it with your whole being - their loss would seem easier to bear. Or did the weekly experience of the Mass just wash over them, deadened as only those who have worked six days a week for many years on end at heavy physical labour can be? With no holiday weeks, how they must have looked forward to the next saint's day, or to the church ales - those village parties held after Mass on certain Sundays in the church - Whitsun for instance - in those years before village halls, when the church congregation and the village population were the same collection of people!

I returned from these musings to the present and to Mr. Chapman's 'little campaign'. Dode's main enemy remains vandalism. The church looks like Fort Knox, surrounded as it is by a high wire fence - a precaution, however inappropriate an impression it may create, which is unfortunately necessary. Not so long ago the church door was destroyed and a new one has had to be built. The only answer, Mr Chapman and his team believe, is permanent occupation. This is why they plan to build a small Retreat building nearby, in which extended periods of prayer and meditation can be held. If, as they hope, groups will regularly come to the house, and people of all faiths and of none are seen to use it, they believe that vandalism (which thrives on being undetected) will eventually vanish.

Only time will tell whether Mr Chapman's work will bear permanent fruit. He himself seems charmingly surprised by the recent publicity and consequent requests to hold prayers or services from a number of religious groups of widely different beliefs. There is no doubt that his campaign has touched some nerve in our worried, vaguely questing, undogmatic age of anxiety. When we drove away to join, all too quickly, the frenetic M2, we knew we would long remember our visit, and the little church on whose site prayers of different faiths have been offered intermittently for 2500 years.

10

THEY CAME to DEAL

ANY VISITOR'S BOOK for Deal must be headed by Julius Caesar. We have no written account of the area earlier than his.

Caesar's landings were conceived as voyages of reconnaissance, which would assist the final occupation of Gaul (France). The people who lived in the region of the Pas de Calais were of the same race as those who inhabited East Kent. They were regularly reinforced by their brethren in East Kent and just as regularly took refuge there when hard pressed. Caesar, a highly successful Roman General with an eye on a political career back home, decided that a landing in strength would put a stop to such interference. He may well have had tentative schemes of extending the Roman Empire's boundaries northwards, but such plans would depend on the ease of conquest, and could be sanctioned only by his political masters.

Caesar's accounts are invariably written with his readers in mind, and his readers were the Roman authorities. He writes of himself in the third person and presents his campaigns in ways favourable to himself. He does all he can to paint a favourable gloss on an enterprise which was in fact a failure.

Caesar's force was formidable. Eighty transport ships carried 10,000 infantrymen across the Channel, escorted by armed galleys. They enjoyed a smooth crossing, embarking from Calais at about midnight on a late August evening. Unfortunately the four thousand cavalry, who embarked separately, never arrived in time for the landing.

Nobody knows exactly where Caesar's men landed. But it seems obvious that the area off which he first anchored his transports was that of the White Cliffs. The beach to which he proceeded 'about seven miles' along the coast was probably Deal beach.

Caesar's First Invasion of Britain, 55BC from Caesar's own account in *The Conquest of Gaul* (Penguin Edition)

'It was now near the end of the summer, and winter sets in early in those parts, because all that coast of Gaul faces north. Nevertheless, Caesar made active preparations for an expedition to Britain, because he knew that in almost all the Gallic campaigns the Gauls had received reinforcements from the Britons. Even if there was not time for a campaign that season, he thought it would be of great advantage to him merely to visit the island, to see what its inhabitants were like, and to make himself acquainted with the lie of the land, the harbours, and the landing-places. Of all this the Gauls knew next to nothing; for in the ordinary way traders are the only people who visit Britain, and even they know only that part of the coast which faces Gaul. And so, although he interviewed traders from all parts, he could not ascertain anything about the size of the island, the character and strength of the tribes which inhabited it, their manner of fighting and customs, or the harbours capable of accommodating a large fleet of big ships. In order to get this information before risking an expedition, he sent a warship in command of Volusenus, whom he considered a suitable man for the job. His orders were to make a general reconnaissance and return as soon as he could. Volusenus reconnoitred the coast as far as he could without disembarking and putting himself into the power of the natives, which he dared not do, and returned four days later with his report.

In due course about eighty transports, which Caesar considered sufficient to convey two legions, were obtained and assembled, and also a number of warships, which were assigned to the quaestor, the generals, and the officers of the auxiliary troops. Besides these there

149

were eighteen transports at a point eight miles along the coast, which were prevented by a contrary wind from making the same harbour as the rest; these were allotted to the cavalry. After the completion of these arrangements, Caesar took advantage of favourable weather and set sail about midnight, ordering the cavalry to proceed to the farther port, embark there, and follow him. As these conducted the operation too slowly, their transports were carried back to land by the tide. Caesar himself reached Britain with the first ships about nine o'clock in the morning, and saw the enemy's forces posted on all the hills. The lie of the land at this point was such that javelins could be hurled from the cliffs right on to the narrow beach enclosed between them and the sea. Caesar thought this a quite unsuitable place for landing, and therefore rode at anchor until three o'clock, in order to give the rest of the ships time to come up. Meanwhile he assembled the generals and military tribunes, and, telling them what he had learned from Volusenus, explained his plans. He warned them that the exigencies of warfare, and particularly of naval operations, in which things move rapidly and the situation is constantly changing, required the instant execution of every order. On dismissing the officers he found that both wind and tidal current were in his favour. He therefore gave the signal for weighing anchor, and after proceeding about seven miles ran his ships aground on a evenly sloping beach, free from obstacles.

The natives, on realizing his intention, had sent forward their cavalry and a number of the chariots which they are accustomed to use in warfare; the rest of their troops followed close behind and were ready to oppose the landing. The Romans were faced with very grave difficulties. The size of the ships made it impossible to run them aground except in fairly deep water; and the soldiers, unfamiliar with the ground, with their hands full, and weighed down by the heavy burden of their arms, had at the same time to jump down from the ships, get a footing in the waves, and fight the enemy, who, standing on dry land or advancing only a short way into the water, fought with all their limbs unencumbered and on perfectly familiar ground, boldly hurling javelins and galloping their horses, which were trained to this kind of work. These perils frightened our soldiers, who were quite unaccustomed to battles of this kind, with the result that they did not show the same alacrity and enthusiasm as they usually did in battles on dry land.

Seeing this, Caesar ordered the warships - which were swifter and easier to handle than the transports, and likely to impress the natives more by their unfamiliar appearance - to be removed a short distance from the others, and then to be rowed hard and run ashore on the enemy's right flank, from which position slings, bows, and artillery could be used by men on deck to drive them back. This manoeuvre was highly successful. Scared by the strange shape of the warships, the motion of the oars, and the unfamiliar machines, the natives halted and then retreated a little. But as the Romans still hesitated, chiefly on account of the depth of the water, the man who carried the eagle of the 10th legion, after praying to the gods that his action might bring good luck to the legion, cried in a loud voice: 'Jump down, comrades, unless you want to surrender our eagle to the enemy; I, at any rate, mean to do my duty to my country and my general'. With these words he leapt out of the ship and advanced towards the enemy with the eagle in his hands.

At this the soldiers, exhorting each other not to submit to such a disgrace, jumped with one accord from the ship, and the men from the next ships, when they saw them, followed them and advanced against the enemy. Both sides fought hard. But as the Romans could not keep their ranks or get a firm foothold or follow their proper standards, and men from different ships fell in under the first standard they came across, great confusion resulted. The enemy knew all the shallows, and when they saw from the beach small parties of soldiers disembarking one by one, they galloped up and attacked them at a disadvantage, surrounding them with superior numbers, while others would throw javelins at the right flank of a whole group. Caesar therefore ordered the warships' boats and the scouting-vessels to be loaded with troops, so that he could send help to any point where he saw the men in difficulties. As soon as the soldiers had got a footing on the beach and had waited for all their comrades to join them, they charged the enemy and put them to flight, but could not pursue very far, because the cavalry had not been able to hold their course and make the island. This was the one thing that prevented Caesar from achieving his usual success.

The defeated enemy, as soon as they rallied after their flight, hastened to send an embassy to ask for peace, promising to give hostages and carry out Caesar's commands. With these envoys came Commius the Atrebatian, whom Caesar had sent on ahead to Britain. When he had disembarked and was delivering Caesar's message to them in the character of an ambassador, the natives had arrested and bound him. Now, after the battle, they sent him back, and in asking for peace threw the blame for this proceeding on the common people, begging Caesar to pardon an error due to ignorance.

Caesar reproached them for making war on him without provocation, after sending envoys to the continent of their own accord to sue for peace, but said that he would pardon their ignorance, and demanded hostages. Some of these they handed over at once; the rest they said would have to be fetched from a distance, and should be delivered in a few days' time. Meanwhile they bade their men return to the fields, and the chiefs began to come from all parts to solicit Caesar's favour for themselves and their tribes. Peace was thus concluded.'

Caesar's description of the people who lived in Deal's interior is a mixture of respect and amusement. These people are certainly not ignorant savages, but their family lives and the way they paint their persons seem strange to the 'civilised' Romans. He continues:

'The interior of Britain is inhabited by people who claim, on the strength of an oral tradition, to be aboriginal; the coast, by Belgic immigrants who came to plunder and make war - nearly all of them retaining the names of the tribes from which they originated - and later settled down to till the soil. The population is exceedingly large, the ground thickly studded with homesteads, closely resembling those of the Gauls, and the cattle very numerous. For money they use either bronze, or gold coins, or iron ingots of fixed weights. Tin is found inland, and small quantities of iron near the coast; the copper that they use is imported. There is timber of every kind, as in Gaul, except beech and fir. Hares, fowl, and geese they think it unlawful to eat, but rear them for pleasure and amusement. The climate is more temperate than in Gaul, the cold being less severe.

The island is triangular, with one side facing Gaul. One corner of this side, on the coast of Kent, is the landing-place for nearly all the ships from Gaul, and points east; the lower corner points south. The length of this side is about 475 miles. Another side faces west, towards Spain. In this direction is Ireland, which is supposed to be half the size of Britain, and lies at the same distance from it as Gaul. Midway across is the Isle of Man, and it is believed that there are also a number of smaller islands, in which according to some writers there is a month of perpetual darkness at the winter solstice. Our inquiries on this subject were always fruitless, but we found by accurate measurements with a water-clock that the nights are shorter than on the continent. This side of Britain, according to the natives' estimate, is 665 miles long. The third side faces north; no land lies opposite it, but its eastern corner points roughly in the direction of Germany. Its length is estimated at 760 miles. Thus the whole island is 1,900 miles in circumference. By far the most civilized inhabitants are those living in Kent (a purely maritime district), whose way of life differs little from that of the Gauls. Most of the tribes in the interior do not grow corn but live on milk and meat, and wear skins. All the Britons dye their bodies with woad, which produces a blue colour, and this gives them a more terrifying appearance in battle. They wear their hair long, and shave the whole of their bodies except the head and the upper lip. Wives are shared between groups of ten or twelve men, especially between brothers and between fathers and sons; but the offspring of these unions are counted as the children of the man with whom a particular woman cohabited first.

In chariot fighting the Britons begin by driving all over the field hurling javelins, and generally the terror inspired by the horses and the noise of the wheels are sufficient to throw their opponents' ranks into disorder. Then, after making their way between the squadrons of their own cavalry, they jump down from the chariots and engage on foot. In the meantime their charioteers retire a short distance from the battle and place the chariots in such a position that their masters, if hard pressed by numbers, have an easy means of retreat to their own lines. Thus they combine the mobility of cavalry with the staying-power of infantry; and by daily training and practice they attain such proficiency that even on a steep incline they are able to control the horses at full gallop, and to check and turn them in a moment. They can run along the chariot pole, stand on the yoke, and get back into the chariot as quick as lightning.'

Caesar's Second Invasion 54 BC

Caesar and his men were to take a closer look at the people of Kent next year, and his account is contained in his 'Conquest of Gaul' (Penguin Edition). He returned, it would seem, at about the same month - late August. He had learned a lesson from his first landing and redesigned his landing ships.

The Mediterranean is tideless, so: 'To enable them to be loaded quickly and beached easily he had them made slightly lower than those which we generally use in the Mediterranean - especially as he had found that owing to the frequent ebb and flow of the tides the waves in the Channel were comparatively small.'

But, rather surprisingly, he still landed at Deal. If his scouts had sailed eastwards along the Kentish coast and found the wonderful natural harbour, as it was then, of Richborough - as the Roman invaders did ninety years later - the whole story would probably have been completely different. As it was the experiences through which he drove his men were similar to those they had suffered last year.

They landed with more than 10,000 infantry and 4,000 cavalry and marched quickly inland to storm the British fortress at Bigbury, near Canterbury. But again, his fleet, drawn up off Deal beach, was badly damaged by storm and he was forced to return there for 10 days to organise repairs. Caesar's description of the beach at Deal is rather puzzling, to those accustomed to its modern shingle. He had been happy, he writes, to leave his ships 'anchored on an open shore of soft sand.'

But when he returned he saw 'with his own eyes' that 'about forty ships were a total loss; the rest looked as if they could be repaired at the cost of much trouble.' He decided that 'although it was a task involving enormous labour . . . it would be best to have all the ships beached and enclosed together with the camp by one fortification.' It took ten days to complete the plan.

Caesar then marched his men far inland, for the local Britons had put all their forces under the command of their compatriot King Cassivellaunus, whose headquarters were at Wheathampstead, near St. Albans. This meant crossing both the Medway and, more formidably, the Thames. The Romans captured Wheathampstead and forced the King's surrender. But Caesar was clearly determined to return to Gaul before the autumn gales. He marched at great speed back to Deal, and crossed the Channel with all his men. He never returned and the Romans left the British alone until the invasion of the Emperor Claudius in AD43, which led to the occupation of Britain until the final withdrawal of the legions in 407.

The Saxon Period

The only evidence available for the years between the departure of the Romans from Richborough in 407 and the invasion of the Normans in 1066 is archaeological. The expert Dr Ivan Green in his *Book of Deal and Walmer* writes:

'There were no natural features here (i.e. at Deal) to facilitate defence, it was always exposed to hit and run or piratical raids by sea, and the land was not so rich as to make its tenure a particularly attractive proposition to those who had a choice of better sites.

Instead, if we can judge from the many and varied artifacts which have come to light, the land here was probably occupied by many separate family groups, cultivating small parcels of land, in trade and cultural matters as much concerned with the continent as they were with other similar communities inland'. The union of Deal with Calais in terms of trade and people thus continued.

Inland, close to Deal, the Anglo-Saxon settlers who occupied Kent from 449 onwards and enslaved the British tribes whom they found in possession of the land, may have formed small villages - around St. Mary's Church at Walmer, for instance, at Upper Deal, and Mongeham. It is not until the Norman settlers assessed Deal and area for taxation purposes in the Domesday Book of 1086 that we possess any firm information.

Norman Deal

The Normans landed at Pevensey in East Sussex in 1066 and won the Battle of Hastings shortly afterwards. They marched along the coast through Deal to Dover and from there, after heavy losses through plague, continued along the old Watling Street to London and Westminster Abbey. By the end of the year Kent was under the same systematic occupation as it experienced during the Roman period. Twenty years later Deal and area was assessed for taxation purposes, along with much of the rest of the country, in the Domesday Book. Its total population, says Dr. Green, 'could have been comfortably accommodated in two motor coaches.'

Domesday, together with the Domesday Monachorum (the Domesday of the monks), shows Deal, Mongeham and Sholden as part of local monastic estates. Deal is under St. Martin's Priory, Dover, while Mongeham and Sholden belong to St. Augustine's, Canterbury.

From the twelfth century onwards Upper Deal began to live two lives. Its people cultivated their strips in the common fields and pastured their animals on the common land. They fulfilled their obligations to their monastic overlords, working on their estates and providing them with the traditional services of labour, food, and animals. But as they grew in numbers they began increasingly to go down to the nearby sea to fish. They built temporary shelters on the beach, and they beat a path from the Centre of Upper Deal, opposite

Saint Leonard's Church, to the sea. The path - Church Path - is much the same still today, until it meets the railway.

Deal Beach

At about this time changes to the seashore gave more opportunities to the town's fishermen, as well as extending the amount of land available to its small farmers. The sandy beach onto which Caesar's men had landed began to disappear. In its place came a great shingle bank, slowly built up, year by year, by the sea. Meanwhile the cultivated land slowly extended towards the sea until it reached the shingle bank which stopped any further progress. Once this land was drained the small farmers profited from the changes as much as the fishermen. Often the two were the same, the strip-farmers spending half their time as fishermen.

The Downs

The same process which was building up the shingle of Deal Beach was gradually blocking the entrances to Dover and Sandwich harbours. Ships bound to and from the Thames estuary and London now began increasingly to use the Downs, the four miles of deep water between the Goodwin Sands and Deal Beach, as an anchorage. At first they merely sheltered there, but after a while they began to take on stores of all sorts - fresh water, anchors, rope and sailcloth and to receive the latest mail. For ships sailing to London - often at the end of long journeys from India and the East - the Downs offered their first opportunity of contact with England before they started on the last lap to London. For outgoing ships Deal was the last port of call before many weary weeks at sea. By the Dissolution of the Monasteries in 1538, when the monks' estates passed to the Crown, Deal's future livelihood as a supplier to ships working one of Europe's busiest trade routes had become clear.

Threats of Invasion

From medieval times Deal had become a 'limb' or subsidiary of Sandwich - one of the original Cinque Ports along with Dover, Hythe, Romney and Hastings. At first, when Sandwich was prosperous, she made few demands on Deal. With Sandwich's decline, she demanded more and more money and sailors to meet her obligations of servicing the Royal Navy. Finally, in 1699, Deal secured its own charter. By that time naval servicing by the Ports had ended.

Henry VIII feared invasion by France, and in 1540 he built, with materials pillaged from Canterbury's Christ Church monastery, Deal Castle, one of the last castles to be built in England. It was designed as an artillery platform, from which guns with a range of about 400 yards could cover the landing beaches. They never fired in anger, any more than those in 1588 did, when invasion by the Spanish Armada was expected. Then the castle was fully garrisoned, and naval ships, anchored in the Downs, were ready for action. Deal had fireships ready to sail across Channel and penetrate the circle of Spanish ships anchored outside Calais. In fact they were not used, eight other fireships doing the damage on the night of August 7-8 which led to the Spanish Armada's flight up the North Sea and round the northern coast of Scotland, never to return.

Celia Fiennes

Celia Fiennes rode over much of England during the years 1685-1705 and kept a diary of what she saw. She came to Kent in the late summer of 1697 and rode to Deal from Dover. She describes her experiences in her 'Journeys.' The description is one long breathless sentence:-

'Thence we went to Deale 7 mile all by the sea side which is called the Downs, which sometymes is full of shipps all along the Road but now there were not many; the Downs seemes to be so open a place and the shoar so easye for landing I should think it no difficulty to land a good army of men in a little tyme, there is only 3 little forts or

Castles they call them, about a miles distance one to another Warworth (Walmer) at Deal and Sandwich, which hold a few Guns but I should think they would be of little effect and give the enemy no great trouble; Deale looks like a good thriveing place the buildings new and neate brickwork with gardens, I believe they are most masters of shipps houses and seamen or else those that belong to the Cordage and saile makeing, with other requisites to shipping, all this Country about seemes to be a very fruitfull soyle and full of woods; you see a many pretty towns altogether almost, neate Churches and towers all the way you travell from Dover to Deale on your left hand, but beyond Deale you go a very deepe heavy sand for 4 mile to Sandwich; you go along by the Sea side in sight of the Isle of Thannet which is just over against Sandwich, and is so neer it you see the land and inclosures and woods and houses - I suppose its not a quarter of a league from Sandwitch - this is a sad old town all timber building, you enter by a gate and so you go out of it by a gate, but its run so to decay that except one or two good houses its just like to drop down the whole town.'

Daniel Defoe

In the early eighteenth century Defoe toured much of England and Wales, noting down his impressions with meticulous care. He was working secretly for the Prime Minister, Robert Harley, and his 'Tour of England and Wales' was not published until the 1720s. He came to Deal from Sandwich, an 'old, decayed, poor, miserable town.'

'From Sandwich to Deal is about six miles. This place is famous for the road for shipping, so well known all over the trading world, by the name of the Downs, and where almost all ships which arrive from foreign parts for London, or go from London to foreign parts, and who pass the Channel, generally stop; the homeward-bound to dispatch letters, send their merchants and owners the good news of their arrival, and set their passengers on shore, and the like; and the outward-bound to receive their last orders,letters, and farewells from owners, and friends, take in fresh provisions, etc.

This place would be a very wild and dangerous road for ships, were it not for the South Foreland, a head of land, forming the east point of the Kentish shore; and is called, the South, as its situation respects the North Foreland; and which breaks the sea off, which would otherwise come rolling up from the west. And yet on some particular winds, and especially, if they over-blow, the Downs proves a very wild road; ships are driven from their anchors, and often run on shore, or are forced on the said sands, or into Sandwich-Bay, or Ramsgate-Peer, as above, in great distress; this is particularly when the wind blows hard at SE or a E by N or ENE and some other points; and terrible havoc has been made in the Downs at such times.

But the most unhappy account that can be given of any disaster in the Downs, is in the time of that terrible tempest, which we call by way of distinction, the Great Storm, being on 27th of November 1703, unhappy in particular; for that there chanced just at that time to be a great part of the royal navy under Sir Cloudesly Shovel, just come into the Downs, in their way to Chatham, to be laid up. There remained in the Downs about twelve sail when this terrible blast began, at which time England may be said to have received the greatest loss that ever happened to the royal navy at one time; either by weather, by enemies, or by any accident whatsoever; the short account of it, as they showed it me in the town, I mean of what happened in the Downs, is as follows.

The 'Northumberland', a third rate, carrying 70 guns, and 353 men; the 'Restoration', a second rate, carrying 76 guns, and 386 men; the 'Sterling-Castle', a second rate, carrying 80 guns, and 400 men, but had but 349 men on board; and the 'Mary' a third rate, of 64 guns, having 273 men on board; these were all lost, with all their men, high and low; except only one man out of the 'Mary', and 70 men out of the 'Sterling-Castle', who were taken up by boats from Deal. All this was besides the loss of merchants' ships, which was exceeding great not here only, but in almost all the ports in the south, and west of England; and also in Ireland, which I shall have occasion to mention again in another place.

From hence we pass over a pleasant champaign country, with the sea, and the coast of France, clear in your view; and by the very gates of the ancient castle (to the town) of Dover. As we go, we pass by Deal Castle, and Sandown Castle, two small works, of no strength by land, and not of much use by sea; but however maintained by the government for the ordinary services of salutes, and protecting small vessels, which can lie safe under their cannon from picaroons, privateers, etc. in time of war.

Neither Dover nor its castle has any thing of note to be said of them, but what is in common with their neighbours; the castle is old, useless, decayed, and serves for little; but to give the title and honour of government to men of quality, with a salary, and sometimes to those that want one. The town is one of the Cinque Ports, sends members to Parliament, who are called barons, and has it self an ill repaired, dangerous, and good for little harbour and pier, very chargeable and little worth. The packets for France go off from here, as also those for Nieuport, with the mails for Flanders, and all those ships which carry freights from New-York to Holland, and from Virginia to Holland, come generally hither, and unlade their goods, enter them with, and show them to the custom-house officers, pay the duties, and then enter them again by certificate, reload them, and draw back the duty by debenture, and so they go away for Holland.

From this place the coast affords nothing of note; but some other small Cinque-Ports, such as Hith and Rumney, and Rye; and as we pass to them Folkstone, eminent chiefly for a multitude of fishing-boats belonging to it, which are one part of the year employed in catching mackerel for the city of London. The Folkstone men catch them, and the London and Barking mackerel-smacks, of which I have spoken at large in Essex, come down and buy them, and fly up to market with them, with such a cloud of canvas, and up so high that one would wonder their small boats could bear it and should not overset.

As I rode along this coast, I perceived several dragoons riding, officers, and others armed and on horseback, riding always about as if they were huntsmen beating up their game; upon inquiry I found their diligence was employed in quest of the owlers, as they call them, and sometimes they catch some of them; but when I came to enquire farther, I found too, that often times these are attacked in the night, with such numbers, that they dare not resist, or if they do, they are wounded and beaten, and sometimes killed; and at other times are obliged, as it were, to stand still, and see the wool carried off before their faces, not daring to meddle.   But I find so many of these desperate fellows are of late taken up, by the courage and vigilance of the soldiers, that the knots are very much broken, and the owling-trade much abated, at least on that side the French also finding means to be supplied from Ireland with much less hazard, and at very little more expense.'

Extracts from the Journal of William Stanton (1803-78), Deal Pilot

When William Stanton was eight, his father, who was doing well, sent him to boarding school at Walmer. Four and a half years later, the source of his father's wealth was revealed. As his son delicately put it, Stanton Senior 'unfortunate in smuggling, got into prison.' All his goods were seized by the Exchequer, and William had to leave school. His superior early education explains the style of his Journal, which is far better written than one would expect from someone who went to sea at twelve.

Times were hard when Stanton left school, and he could not find a job for a while. Then one evening when he was walking along Deal Beach 'with my shoes slung over my shoulders, there came two men down to a vessel's boat, which lay along shore. One of the men asked me my name, and on my telling him, he put me in his boat and took me on board his vessel, a small fore and aft schooner called the 'Nancy' of Deal. We weighed and made sail for Ostend which they reached the next day. A week later they sailed for Folkestone, just the two of them, the Captain and himself, with cargo, some part of which was 'concealed', some not. Stanton had joined the large number of men in Deal who plied the cross-channel trade with goods, some of which were 'concealed' and some not. One suspects the main concentration was on the former.

After a few more trips of this nature Stanton joined an enterprise which promised to provide Deal with a steady source of legal employment for the indefinite future. If, indeed, they had been successful the whole nature of Deal would have changed. Deal would have become another Hull. Stanton describes the activities of the Iceland Cod Fishery, 'a company formed in 1816 by public subscription, likewise all the vicinity; everybody subscribed liberally as it seemed to be an important benefit to the town of Deal for the future.'

Two sloops and a schooner set sail for Iceland. 'Captain Thomas had the offer of one of the sloops, which he accepted, and took me with him, each vessel to carry ten men and four boys . . . We soon arrived out on the fishing grounds, close under the high land of Iceland, where Mount Hecla is your constant companion by night and day, with its awful grand appearance; the sun also to be seen all night, although so bitterly cold, and the mountains all covered with snow - a most dreary looking place. On our visiting the shore for water, we found the inhabitants scarce, and in the most abject state of poverty, disease and misery, and covered with vermin, so that we could not allow them to come on board. They fed on fish, without either bread or salt - their dreadful state I can scarcely describe.

One morning early there was a man brought his boy alongside, the boy had a gathering on his finger. It had bursted and he wanted something to put to it. I gave him some burnt loaf sugar, lint, rag and salve, and made him understand which way to use it. On my going on shore some time after I saw the boy, and his finger was quite well. His mother was standing close to him, when she threw her arms round my neck and kissed me in a most grateful manner. And this boy was the Governor's son, named Johnson. This will show you the dreadfully distressed state they must have been in at that date.

We finished the voyage in about six months. Our vessel, the 'Prosperity,' did tolerably well, but the schooner 'Apollo' and 'Sister' sloop did very badly, so that put a death-blow to the concern; the company then tried the herring fishery, by curing for exportation. But after the remittances came from abroad, the parties employed as 'treasurers' absconded with the cash, thus ending a speculation which bid so well for the future welfare of Deal in *felo-de-se*.'

Voyage To India

In the month of December 1819, Stanton, now aged sixteen, went to London to join the 'Lady Lushington,' 800 tons. They were bound for Calcutta, touching at Madeira and Madras. At Madras they loaded salt for Calcutta, but ran aground on the way. 'It was about 3 am, dismal dark, the sea breaking most furiously over us ... At daylight a most awful thing presented itself as eyes ever witnessed - men, women and children in their nightclothes, shrieking most piteously, and all the rigging lying across the decks; people washing down the main hatchway, guns all adrift, danger and death staring on you on all sides. A tremendous sea came and swept the poop clean off her. The captain, then addressing us, wished every sailor to do his best to make a raft for the 'females.' We, with the greatest difficulty, succeeded in getting it over the side. After getting it clear of the wreck to the quarter, to get the females on it, the chief mate cut the rope, and away he went, with only 4 male passengers - we never got a female on it. The villain thought he had left us to perish! The raft was large enough to carry every soul on board.

I then began to think of trying for myself. A man begged me to take his little boy with me, as I prepared to swim ashore. Then a heavy sea came and took us all overboard. On my coming to the surface of the water, I caught the boy on my shoulder - the father sank to rise no more.'

Stanton swam ashore, while the boy was taken ashore by catamaran. Stanton does not make it clear whether the catamaran was sailed by a native or by a member of the crew who had already struggled ashore.

'I unbuttoned my trousers, and kicked them off, to swim the better, being now naked. I then fell in with a boat, bottom up. I got on it for a rest. I had not been there long before a heavy sea came and washed me off it; it was like a nutmeg grater the boat's bottom was so rough, and I could not hold on to it, for it cut me in several places so dreadfully, the scars of which I retain to this day. After the greatest of difficulty I reached the shore, but too feeble even to crawl, and being full of water. A native came to me and behaved very kind, and rubbed my stomach until he got the water out of me, and lent me his only bit of clothing he had.'

Twenty five of the passengers and crew were drowned, and forty five saved.

Stanton and a friend now made for Calcutta by land. After three days they came to a large jungle.

'While getting along the length of this jungle, the mixture of sounds from birds and beasts of all sorts were curious harmony indeed, more particularly the jackals, whose dismal howling was anything but pleasant. After rounding the end of the jungle we heard a somewhat louder howling than was common, which we were satisfied was a tiger.

I said to Tom it is of no use running. With that he held out his hand, and said it was the hand of a man and a Scotchman - we will live or die together! By this time it was drawing very near, when, as God would have it, we came to a river, when Tom exclaimed he could not swim. I told him I would never leave him, and if he would take it calmly and place his left arm on my back, I would swim him across the river, which I accomplished very well indeed. We stood still, and saw by the moon the tiger as plain as possible. He came up to his middle in the water, and gave some tremendous howls. I did not know at that time that tigers would take the water, which was a good job, as it would have robbed me of my consolation of being safe after getting across the river.'

Stanton and Tom made their way to Calcutta, and thence home. They remained 'like two brothers up to the day of his death.'

Stanton's next voyage was to South America, but when he returned to Deal he bought a lugger, the 'Ox.' The luggers or hovellers as the introduction to Stanton's Journal describes them,

'were constantly being launched to render assistance to any . . . craft . . . in distress, and Deal, being opposite the dreaded Goodwin

Sands, there was no lack of shipping requiring assistance; replacing lost anchors and cables, piloting the ship of some bewildered master through a swatchway amid the surf, into the comparative safety of the Downs.

Night and day the lugger was kept ready to be launched. With bows pointing seawards, she was poised on the steep upper part of Deal Beach, and kept from running down by a slip chain. When about to launch, lengths of greased plank were laid at intervals down the beach, and the last wood, as the planks were called, was dropped in the surf as she took to the water.'

Deal gained a good income from such servicing. The lugger's crew numbered up to 10 men, and they were paid on a 'no wreck, no pay' basis.

In 1865 the first lifeboat was stationed on Deal beach. Before this the Deal luggers did all the rescue work on the Goodwins. Two years later Stanton's last entry reads:-

'May 12, 1867. Standing first for shore duty at 7.30pm . . . I met with a most serious accident, which dislocated my ankle, which incapacitated me from duty.

After eight months . . . I appealed for superannuation, March 3rd 1868. It was granted. I gave up my licence and was pensioned at £50 per annum, minus £6 per year taxation . . . May it please God to give me health to enjoy it.'

He took up cobbling boots and shoes in his retirement, but suffered from asthma, and died in 1878.

William Cobbett (1763-1835)

When you read William Cobbett's many writings, particularly his *Rural Rides*, you realise how much there is to be said for not going to University. Cobbett, like George Orwell and Daniel Defoe, writes simple, direct and clear English without qualifications or elaborations - and all three never went near a university. Cobbett also is particularly glad that he never attended one of those 'dens of dunces, Westminster and Winchester.' He ran away from home at the age of eight and later joined the Army in North America. Before and after the wars with France, Cobbett toured England on his horse, recording what he saw in his *Political Register*, the first popular newspaper in England, and in his *Rural Rides*.

His prejudices were many and violent. Above all he hated successive English governments who had set out, as he saw it, to ruin small farmers like himself and had wasted taxpayer's money by waging utterly unnecessary wars with France. Deal was a place whose soldiers, sailors and inhabitants were deeply involved in those wars and so became the target of one of his most splenetic attacks when he rode through it in September 1823.

'Deal is a most villainous place. It is full of filthy looking people. Great desolation of abomination has been going on here; tremendous barracks, partly pulled down and partly tumbling down, and partly occupied by soldiers. Everything seems upon the perish. I was glad to hurry along through it, and to leave its inns and public-houses to be occupied by the tarred, and trowsered, and blue-and-buff crew whose very vicinage I always detest. From Deal you come along to Upper Deal, which, it seems, was the original village; thence upon a beautiful road to Sandwich, which is a rotten borough. Rottenness, putridity is excellent for land, but bad for boroughs. This place, which is as villainous a hole as one would wish to see, is surrounded by some of the finest land in the world. Along on one side of it lies a marsh. On the other sides of it is land which they tell me bears seven quarters of wheat to an acre. It is certainly very fine; for I saw large pieces of radish-seed on the roadside; this seed is grown for the seedsmen in London; and it will grow on none but rich land. All the corn is carried here except some beans and some barley.'

Deal as a 'Watering-Place'

The 'Golden Age of Deal' ended, as we have seen, with the conclusion of Napoleonic wars. Like William Stanton's father, many townsmen and shopkeepers now became bankrupt. Smuggling was increasingly harassed, and only a few families possessed luggers, which provided a precarious enough trade. A group of townsmen began the campaign to make Deal a 'watering-place,' along the lines of Ramsgate or Margate. If they were to achieve their ambition three improvements were vital. Deal must build itself a pier, it must offer public baths and a reading room, and it must attract better public transport.

The lack of a harbour at Deal had always severely limited the town's volume of trade - an argument which the Act of 1838, which sanctioned the formation of a Deal Pier Company, recognised. The act authorised the building of a wooden pier or jetty so that passengers and light cargo could land without having to take a small boat. The pier was 250 feet long, and the plan was to double its length. That project never received the necessary money or enthusiasm. The violence of the winter winds removed parts of the pier regularly, until in 1857 the whole pier collapsed under the attack of a south-eastern gale. Seven years later a much stronger and more confident pier, the Iron Pier, was built which lasted until the Second World War. It too was damaged by storms, and finally demolished. The present pier was opened by the Duke of Edinburgh in 1957, the last pier to be built in Britain.

The Victorians were sold on the benefits which would inevitably follow, in Deal as elsewhere, the construction of a pier. The whole magnificent idea of a seafront raised on wooden columns, deeply implanted on the sea bed and extending for up to a mile in length appealed to them. Not only could promenaders stroll along it, fishermen fish from it, and ships unload at it. You could look back from the pier's end and study the town from the depths of the sea in comfort. Here was one more triumph of man over nature, a particularly jaunty 'improvement.' Two years after the final collapse of the wooden pier, a visitor to Deal is taunting the townspeople with their conservatism:

'Sir,

I am not a native of your town, but I have been in it long enough to observe that it is half a century behind most watering-places . . . Dover and Ramsgate can boast of their artificial harbours, and Margate of its piers, and also of their numerous lodging houses, from their elegant and commodious terraces . . . down to the humble cottage, where the shopman or artisan may enjoy his annual holiday. To such attractions as these Deal has no pretence . . . With the exception of three gingerbread castles and an irregular range of antiquated buildings, Deal sea frontage is as innocent of the crime of improvement as when Julius Caesar landed, nineteen centuries ago.

Now, Sir, these things need not be . . . Why not form a company for the erection of an Iron Pier? You would soon find it necessary to alter and increase the number of lodging houses; trade in general would flourish and be the making of the town.' (Letter to *Deal, Walmer and Sandwich Telegram*, 6 April 1859. Quoted *Kentish Sources* IX, Kent Archives Office, 1985, p.39.) Five years later, in 1864, the Iron Pier was built.

Deal had long been proud of its bathing machines. Only a few years after the first machines had been introduced at Margate, the first in the country in Margate's opinion, though Brighton did not agree, Dr. Richard Pococke in his *Travels Through England* was noting:

'Dover, Sept. 12, 1754.

At Deal . . . is the original NEW-INVENTED MACHINE for Bathing in the Sea. The Machine moves on 4 wheels, on which is erected a commodious Dressing-Room, furnished in a genteel Manner. This Machine is so contrived that the Persons who bathe descend from out of the above Room into a Bath, which forms itself in the natural Sea 7 Feet in Length and 5 Feet in Breadth; all inclosed and railed, which renders it both secure and private.

. . . NB A proper Woman is provided to attend the Ladies if required.' (*Travels Through England* of Dr Richard Pococke, Camden Society II, 1889, 1891.) Quoted *Kentish Sources* VIII, ps.186-7.

Another traveller, William Miller, enthused about the sea bathing, shortly after the Iron Pier had been opened. (I wonder if he had ever himself taken a dip from that shingle, so agonising to bare feet.)

'The air is very salubrious and dry, and the beach being of shingle, the water is beautifully clear and well-suited for bathing; many invalids as well as pleasure seekers have a preference for Deal from the animated sea-view - its fine bathing and invigorating atmosphere,

although it cannot afford the attractions of more fashionable watering places, compensated for, however, by moderate charges and extreme civility.'
(William Miller, *Jottings of Kent*, London 1864. Quoted *Kentish Sources* IX, Kent Archives Office, 1985. p.50.)

The Royal Adelaide Baths and Reading Room, in Beach Street, had been established well before the first pier. It consisted of 'spacious reading-room, library and baths, comprising warm shower and cold baths, and a plunging bath in the basement. There are also a number of bathing machines on the beach, belonging to the same proprietor.'
(S Bagshaw *Directory of Kent*, II, Sheffield 1847, p.355. Quoted in *Kent Sources* VIII, p.174.)

The Baths were built in 1835-6 at the cost of £3000. They do not seem to have been popular, and were sold, six years later, for £1000. They were still going strong in 1847, but never achieved the popularity for which their founders had hoped. No doubt, if they had, assembly rooms, as in Margate, would have followed and perhaps even a theatre, as at Margate or Canterbury. That they did not is an illustration of the failure of Deal to establish itself as a 'Tunbridge Wells by the sea,' the aim of most South Coast promoters.

In 1847 the South Eastern and London and Chatham railways opened a branch line from Minster to Deal, thus connecting Deal with Canterbury West and eventually Charing Cross. But the line between Deal and Dover was not opened till 1881. Even then no cheap daily excursion tickets were issued to Deal, as they long had been to their neighbours - an omission which prompted a petition to the Mayor from Deal Tradesmen, eight years later, written in the plaintive and rather self-piteous tone we have come to expect from those who plead Deal's cause: '. . . For some reasons the Borough of Deal has been excluded from the cheap daily excursions which have been extended to other Watering Places on the South Eastern and Chatham Railways. We have been entirely isolated from receiving benefits not only by money spent by excursionists but totally ignoring our town, one of the prettiest Watering Places on the Coast of Kent.'

By the turn of the century cheap excursions to Deal could be bought.

The superior attitude which the railways adopted to Deal did not in fact make Deal isolated from the rest of the south coast towns or from visitors further afield. As early as 1792 'The Dover and Deal Directory and Guide' was reporting:-

'DEAL - A diligence sets off every morning at nine o'clock to Canterbury, where it waits till the arrival of the coaches from London and returns the same evening. A waggon for luggage goes to Canterbury to meet the London waggon every Monday and Friday, and returns the next day . . .' (*Kentish Archives* VIII - p.34)

The eight o'clock London coach was advertised as reaching Canterbury around 4.30 p.m., so a traveller could breakfast in London and eat his evening meal in Deal without too much strain.

The town relied far more on land communication for its visitors than on transport by sea, though once the wooden jetty was built at Deal pier, ships carrying passengers from Margate and Ramsgate, tied up there. *The Times* of 7 July 1814 advertises a fashionable run by the Princess of Wales Yacht which took in 'Ramsgate, Sandwich, Deal and the adjacent villages,' with 'Capt. Gore or Mr Palmer, Master, attending on board. Passengers could be picked up at the Monument Coffee-house, Fish-street-hill and the Newcastle Coffee-house near Billingsgate. It left Custom House Quay in the Port of London on Fridays and returned on Tuesday morning.'
(Quoted *Kentish Sources* VIII, p.52.)

The class of passenger which the Yacht was hoping to attract was clearly far superior to that carried by the sloops which ran from the London Custom House to Margate and back. In 1763 the sloops and hoys which plied this trade were said to carry:

'a motley crew, of all ages, tempers and dispositions.' 'High and Low, Rich and Poor, Sick and Sound are here indiscriminately blended together.'
(John Lyons, *A Description of the Isle of Thanet*, 1763, *Kentish Sources* VIII, p.49.)

The main challenger to the coach as a means of communication with Deal was 'the steamboat service . . .' The steamboat service from London to Herne Bay was available from 1835 onwards. It claimed to be 'much the cheapest and most agreeable journey to Dover or Deal, as the whole expense from the metropolis to Dover or Deal is 10s.6d; being 5s.6d to land at Herne Bay, 1s.6d by coach to Canterbury and 3s.6d by coach or van from Canterbury to Dover; while the expense, outside the coach from London to Dover is 16s, and inside 30s.'

(*Picture of The New Town of Herne Bay*, 1835, quoted *Archives* VIII, p.74.)

Whatever social aspirations Deal may have entertained at one time, by the turn of the century the town had settled, in its promotion literature, on being the ideal spot for a quiet family holiday. Later, in 1926, the Southern Railway Company's guide to seaside resorts in *Lovely Kent* strikes much the same note. Whereas Tankerton is described as 'Whitstable's select quarter,' Herne Bay as a 'recognised 'week-end resort'', and Margate is singled out for its 'atmosphere of cheerfulness,' Deal is just 'amply endowed with natural and other forms of amusement. Aquatic sports are held weekly in the summer.' (*Kentish Sources* IX, p.140.) The same is true today, with the town being famous only for its week-end angling competitions, straight off the seashore, in the summer.

A wreck on the Goodwins

Wrecks

We have already seen the work of the Deal luggers in connection with William Stanton. The luggers were ready, twenty four hours round and seven days a week, to come to the assistance of ships in distress on the Goodwin Sands, or in between the Goodwins and Deal Beach. There was no lifeboat before 1865, and before then all the rescue work in that area of tumultuous seas was done by the luggers. Their life and work was described by the Reverend T. Stanley Treanor, Chaplain to the Missions to Seamen, Deal and the Downs, in his books *Heroes of the Goodwin Sands* and *The Cry From the Sea*. Treanor went out with the boats in all weathers and was clearly an excellent seaman, as well as a devoted chaplain to his flock, eager to hold services on board ships suffering every type of distress.

Here he is describing the wrecks which formed such an extra and terrible danger to their work, especially at night. They are to be found on pages 22-24, 29-32, and 94-100 of Treanor's *Heroes of the Goodwin Sands.*

'Independently of the breakers and cross-seas of stormy weather, the dangers of the Goodwin Sands arise from the facts that they lie right in the highway of shipping, that at high water they are concealed from view, being then covered by the sea to the depth of from ten to twenty-five feet, varying in different places, and that furious currents run over and around them.

Add to this that they are very lonely and distant from the mainland, and, being surrounded by deep water, are far from help; whilst, as an additional and terrible danger, here and there on the sands, wrecks, anchors, stumps, and notably the great sternpost of the 'Terpsichore,' from which a few months ago Roberts and the Deal lifeboatmen had rescued all the crew, stick up over the surface. And woe be to the boat or vessel which strikes on these!

On September 12, 1891, on my way to the North Sandhead lightship, which, however, we failed to reach by reason of the strong ebb tide against us and the wind dropping to a calm, we revisited this sternpost of the 'Terpsichore.' We got down mast and sails and took to our oars. The light air from the north-east blew golden feathery cloud-films across the great blue arch above our heads, and for once in the arctic summer of 1891 the air was warm and balmy. Starting from the North-west Goodwin buoy, we soon rowed into shallow water, crossing a long spit of sand on which, not far from us, a feathery breaker raced. Again we got into deep water, having just hit the passage into an amphitheatre in the Goodwins of deep water bordered by a circle or ridge of sand about three feet under water, over which the in-tide was fiercely running and rippling, and upon which here and there a breaker raised its warning crest.

We reached the great sternpost of the lost 'Terpsichore' at 9.22am, just two hours before low water at the neap tides, and found it projected five feet nine inches above the water, which was ten feet six inches deep in the swilly close to it, but nowhere shallower than eight feet within a distance of fifty yards from the stump. Underneath in the green sea-water there lay quite visible the keel and framework of the vessel; and again I heard the story from Roberts, the coxswain of the Deal lifeboat, who was with me, of the rescue of the crew of this very vessel at 2.15am on the stormy night of the preceding November 14.

As we held by the green sea-washed stump, it was hard to realise the sublime story of that awful night: the mighty sea warring with the furious wind, and the dismantled, beaten ship - masts gone overboard and tossing in mad confusion of spars and cordage along her side - into which most black and furious hell the lifeboatmen dared to venture the Deal lifeboat, and out of which she and her gallant crew came, by God's mercy, triumphant and unscathed, having saved every soul on board, and also, with a fine touch of humanity often to be found in a brave sailor's heart, the 'harmless, necessary cat' belonging to the vessel. I can assure my readers that poor pussy's head and green eyes peering out of the arms of one of the storm-battered sailors as they struggled up Deal beach was a beautiful and most touching sight.

On this north-west part of the Goodwins, on which hours of the deepest interest could be spent, you can walk a distance of at least two miles, but you are separated by the great north-east swatch of deep water from getting to the extensive north-east jaw on the other side of the swatch, which is also full of wrecks, and round and along the edges of which, on the calmest day, somehow the surf and breakers for ever roar. The southern part of the Goodwins is also full of memories, and of countless wrecks. The ribs of the 'Ganges', the 'Leda', the 'Paul Boyton', the 'Sorrento', all lie there deep down beneath the Sands, excepting when some mighty storm shifts the sand and reveals their skeletons. Deep, too, in the bosom of the Goodwins, masts alone projecting, is settling down the 'Hazelbank', wrecked there in October, 1890; but this southern part at lowest tide is barely uncovered by the sea, and only just awash.

At high water the depth is about three fathoms, varying of course in patches, over this southern part or tail of the sea-monster. It is clear that, being thus, even at low tide, nearly always covered with water, and as the sand when thus covered is much more 'quick' and movable, the southern part of the Goodwins is an exceedingly awkward place to explore. If you made a stumble, as the sands slide under your feet, it might, shall I say, land you into a pit or 'fox-fall,' circular in shape, and very deep. The stumps of forgotten wrecks are also a real danger to the boat which accompanies the investigator.

175

As to the depth of the great sandbank, borings have been made down to the chalk to a depth of seventy-eight feet.

The ships wrecked on the Goodwins go down into it very slowly, but they sometimes literally fall off the steep outer edge into the deep water above described.

One still bright autumn morning I witnessed a tragedy of that description. On the forenoon of November 30, 1888, I was on the deck of a barque, the 'Maritzburg', bound to Port Natal. I had visited the men in the forecastle, and indeed all hands fore and aft, as Missions to Seamen chaplain; and to them all I spoke, and was, in fact, speaking of that only 'Name under heaven whereby we must be saved,' when my eyes were riveted, as I gazed right under the sun, by the drama being enacted away to the southward.

There I saw, three miles off, our two lifeboats of Kingsdown and Walmer, each in tow of a steamer which came to their aid, making for the Goodwins, and on the outer edge of the Goodwins I beheld a hapless brig, with sails set, aground. I saw her at that distance lifted by the heavy sea, and at that distance I saw the great tumble of the billows. That she had heavily struck the bottom I also saw, for crash! - and even at that distance I verily seemed to hear the crash - away went her mainmast over her side, and the next instant she was gone, and had absolutely and entirely disappeared. I could not believe my eyes, and rubbed them and gazed again and yet again.

She had perished with all hands. The lifeboats, fast as they went, were just too late, and found nothing but a nameless boat, bottom upwards, and a lifebelt, and no one ever knew her nationality or name. She had struck the Goodwins, and had been probably burst open by the shock, and then, dragged by the great offtide to the east, had rolled into the deep water outside the Goodwins and close to its dreadful edge.'

As an example of a Deal lugger's work as described by Stanley Treanor I have chosen the night of January 26, 1884, and the wreck of the 'Edina.'

'The Edina was one of the great fleet of ships at anchor in the Downs on January 26, 1884. Hundreds of vessels were there straining at their anchors - vessels of many nations, and of various rigs. There were picturesque red-sailed barges anchored close in shore, while even there the sea flew over them. Farther out were Italians, Norwegians and Yankees, all unmistakable to the practised eye; French *chasse-marees*, Germans, Russians and Greeks were there; and each vessel was characterised by some nautical peculiarity. Of course the greater number were our own English vessels, as plainly to be pronounced British as ever was John Bull in the midst of Frenchmen or Spaniards.

It was blowing a heavy gale from the WSW, and towards night, accompanied by furious rain-squalls and thunder, the gale increased to a storm. The most powerful luggers along the beach tried to launch, but as the tide was high they had not run enough to get sufficient impetus, and were therefore beaten back on the beach by the surf.

Some vessels were blown clean out of the Downs, and away from their anchors. Indeed, when the weather cleared between the squalls, a pitiable number of blue light signals of distress were seen in the distance beyond the North Foreland. And it is probable that vessels were lost that night on the Goodwins of which no one has ever heard.

When the tide fell, about 8.45, flares and rockets were seen coming from the Brake, a very dangerous and partially rocky 'Sand' lying close to the Goodwin Sands. Then the Gull lightship also fired guns and rockets. There being obviously a vessel in danger on or near either the Goodwins or the Brake Sand, the Deal lifeboat bell was rung; and a crew was obtained out of the hundred men who rushed to get a place. The beach was smoothed to give the lifeboat a run, she was let go, and, in contrast with the failure of other boats, launched successfully. In receiving the report of the coxswain next day, I asked him what time precisely he launched. Now that evening, about 9 p.m., I was sitting in my own house listening to the long-protracted roar of the wind, and just when I thought the strong walls could bear no more, there came a blinding flash of lightning which paled the lamps, almost simultaneously with a peal of thunder that made the foundations of the house tremble. When I asked the coxswain next day what time exactly he launched, his reply was, 'Just in that clap of thunder.'

This may help my readers to depict the scene in its appalling grandeur, and to realise the meaning of the words, 'A vessel in distress,' and the launch of the lifeboat on its sacred errand.

The flares which had been burning now suddenly stopped. This, however, was owing to the distressed vessel having exhausted her stock of rockets and torches.

Passing under the stern of a schooner which they hailed, the gallant lifeboat crew were pointed out the vessel that had been burning them, riding with a red light in her rigging to attract notice. Making for her, they anchored as usual ahead, and veered down eighty fathoms. In the gale and heavy sea they found the anchor would not hold, and they had to bend on another cable, and pay out a hundred fathoms, and at last they got alongside.

The captain cried out, 'Come on board and save the vessel! My crew are all gone!' And indeed she was in a sore plight.

That evening after dark, about 6pm, this brig, the 'Edina', had been riding out the gale in the Downs. In a furious blast a heavy sea broke her adrift from her anchor, and she came into helpless collision with a ship right astern of her. Grinding fiercely into this other very large vessel, the 'Edina' tore herself free with loss of bowsprit and jib-boom, all her fore-rigging being in dire ruin and confusion.

In the collision, six of the crew of the 'Edina' jumped from her rigging to the other ship with which they were in collision, leaving only three men, the captain, mate, and boy, on board the 'Edina.' By great efforts they, however, were able to let go another anchor, but that did not bite, and the 'Edina' kept dragging with the wreckage and wild tangle of bowsprit and jib-boom hanging over her bows and beating against her side.

One of the six men who had jumped from the 'Edina' in the panic of the collision had, alas! jumped too short, and had fallen between the two vessels. The next day his body was found by the lifeboatmen entangled in the wreckage, and under the bows of the 'Edina.'

The 'Edina' in her wrecked and crippled condition had dragged till she got to the very edge of the Brake Sand. She had dragged for two miles, and at last her anchor held fast when within twenty fathoms or forty yards of the Brake Sand. She was stopped just short of destruction as the sea was breaking heavily under her stern, and had she drifted a few more yards she would have struck the deadly Brake, and have perished with those on board before the lifeboat could have reached her.

In setting off his rockets, the unfortunate captain had blown away a piece of his hand, and was in much suffering, when the advent of the lifeboat proclaimed that he was not to be abandoned to destruction. The vessel was riding in only three fathoms of water, and as a furious sea was running, she was plunging bows under. Six of the lifeboatmen sprang on board and turned to clearing the wreck - the remainder of the men remaining in the lifeboat, as they feared every moment the ship would break adrift and strike.

They worked with the energy of men working for life, but they took three hours to clear away the wreck; this being absolutely necessary in order to get at the windlass and raise the anchor. At morning dawn they found the body of the poor sailor who had failed to spring to the other vessel; they got up anchor, they set the sails, and they brought the vessel out of her dangerous position into Ramsgate Harbour.

That day four weeks the 'Edina' came out of Ramsgate refitted and ready for her voyage to Pernambuco.

Captain Holmes of the 'Cimba'

Captain James Holmes, Master of the 'Cimba', one of the last wool clippers, and of other round-the-world sailing ships, was born in Deal in 1855. He obtained his Master's Certificate in 1882 and became master of the 'Cimba' thirteen years later. According to *The Deal, Walmer, Sandwich and East Kent Mercury* of June 1936 the 'Cimba' was famous for her speed. Once she passed 'The Cutty Sark' the fastest ship of her time, without difficulty.

The 'Mercury' describes Holmes as 'a small, quiet modest man, with a passion for painting ships and growing flowers at sea . . .' In his day he had a reputation for carrying on sail to an extent which alarmed a good many of his crew, and of sparing neither ship nor man. But they never knew him lose his temper, were intensely proud of having served under his command, and shipped with him again and again. In the evening of his days, his bungalow on Shooters Hill, named after the 'Cimba,' was the Mecca of old-time sailing ship men, including a large number of his old apprentices who had risen to high position'.

He died in May 1932, aged 75, and was buried in Deal Cemetery.

He left behind him paintings of all the ships in which he sailed, and his memories, which were published in the 'Mercury' four years later. I have chosen extracts from them, which now follow:-

'The last half century has seen many changes in our national life, yet none is more startling than the passing of the British sailing ship; and this is the more extraordinary in that it was not the slow transition of time, but a complete metamorphose. During the lifetime of men to whom the word 'ship' signified a thing of beauty and white spread sails, that form of vessel has been replaced by a mechanical contrivance without a stitch of canvas. So that whereas twenty, or even twelve years ago, British sailing ships carried the 'red duster' proudly into every part of the world, today there is not one deep sea sailing ship under that flag. They pass before us in a vision of time, a long procession of increasing stateliness and power, culminating in that perfect work of man, the British sailing ship of the late seventies. Then in the height of their pride and perfection, they have passed completely. The moment of their departure was unnoticed, but their glory was undimmed. They continued to make fine passages, they fought for every inch through the fury of the gale, when the world had ceased to mark their exploits, and bets were no longer taken on the date of their arrival.

With the object of preserving the memory of those glorious ships of yesterday, I have painted all those in which I sailed between 1869 and 1921. And for the life on board them let memory recall the days that were.

I cannot say I chose the sea as a career. That was done for me before I was born. All my ancestors were sailors from Deal and Dover. My father, grandfather, and great-grandfather were Cinque Ports pilots. All my contemporary relatives were sailors, or married to sailors, so my intention of going to sea was formed with my first dawn of consciousness; and looking back now, over 74 years, I know that if I had to choose again, I should choose the same. A ship may be a hard mistress, but her fascination is not to be denied, and time cannot dim it.

My First Ship

So it came to pass that at the age of 14 years I joined the barque 'Talavera.' She was a wooden barque of 384 tons register with a figure head of the Duke of Wellington, and was built in Dundee in 1858 for Messrs. Manning and Anderton, of London. She was a regular West Indian trader, loading sugar at St Kitts at Christmas and reaching London the following March, and those months were a nightmare of starvation.

The tea I poured into my numbed little body that first night at sea made me heave my inside up. I think it was concocted from coir and broom bristles, but it never owned a tea leaf. I served all my four years' apprenticeship on cold water, except when we could steal a cup of coffee from the cabin coffee-pot. Bread we never saw. The biscuits could only be broken with a belaying pin, and they had weevils in them. We boys sometimes made amusement for ourselves by organizing races between each other's weevils. The salt beef had to be chopped through like a block of mahogany, and the salt pork, streaked with green, could be smelt all over the ship when the first cask was broached.

Well do I remember the morning we arrived in London. The overlooker was awaiting us. As he came aboard he said 'Had any breakfast?' knowing I had had none for about 150 days, and adding 'Go ashore and get some' as he gave me half-a-crown. And all that half-crown, plus a shilling of my own, went on one glorious feed!

The 'Blair Athol.'

As this trip was intended as a trial before my apprenticeship, it is perhaps unnecessary to remark that I did not repeat it, but was apprenticed next December in the 'Blair Athol,' which if not better, was perhaps not quite so bad. She was a wooden barque of 443 tons register, built in 1863 at Shoreham, and was the biggest vessel belonging to that then busy little port, for Shoreham could boast 350 brigs and barques built for the Mediterranean trade. She was a Mediterranean and Black Sea trader, named after a Derby winner, on which her owner, Mr T F Gates, won the money to build her. She was a nice looking ship, with a Highlander as figurehead, and built of mahogany from a wrecked ship's cargo.

But of her skipper, Captain X, the best thing I can say of him is that he was the worst man I ever sailed under - a drunken, bullying, callous brute, without nerve or conscience. I first made his acquaintance two days after leaving Troon on a freezing December day with the ship beating through a gale. It was my watch below, and, coming out of the house to fetch my dinner from the galley, I saw the old man on the poop talking to the senior apprentice, Pat. He beckoned me aft. 'Here,' he said to Pat, taking a scarf from his neck. 'You go up the weather side to the mizzen truck and tie this scarf on for a vane, and come down the lee side.' 'And you,' he said turning to me, 'Go up the lee side and see he makes it fast properly, and come down the weather side.'

Of course he was drunk, for even a brute will scarcely risk the murder of two boys merely for a mad whim. But orders, drunken or sober, had to be obeyed - as on another occasion, when in a maudlin state, he upset a bucket of water in his lavatory. Finding the floor awash, he yelled to the Mate 'Man the pumps, you d---- fool! Can't you see the ship's sinking?' So the ship's crew worked the pumps all night, to the accompaniment of his tearful cries and curses.

The next trip we made from S. Shields to Alexandria, the Black Sea, and the Sea of Azov, reaching the latter in the depth of winter. And here we suffered all that a Russian winter and a brutal skipper could inflict upon us. We lay 17 miles off the port, inside a 14ft. bar, and we poor devils of boys had to row the Old Man ashore each day and wait for him till 2am, shivering in an open boat, and clad only in dungarees, for the old demon would not let us wear a jersey or monkey jacket even in the boat. And at sea, with a temperature at freezing point, we poor, starved, shivering little wretches, 15 years old, had to take our trick at the wheel without as much as a pair of mittens, at the sight of which he would land us a clout that sent us staggering across the deck.

The first day we took the Old Man ashore at Berdianski might well have been the last. The bo'sun and I ran him in in the long boat and then waited by the boat through the long hours of a freezing afternoon and evening. The bo'sun, to while away the time, chummed up with an Italian boat's crew near by, and as they had a keg of vodki in their boat to warm them the bo'sun also was soon warm and happy. About midnight a Russian came down to the shore and said 'Cap'en say go aboard now and come for him to-morrow.' But by that time the happy bo'sun lay in the bottom of the boat, dead to the world, so the unhappy boy had to hoist the sails singlehanded, sail but 17 miles in freezing wind, and find the ship in the darkness. When I did find her I could awaken no response from her, and despite my frantic yelling and screaming, I was blown away several miles astern. Then I had to beat up again, and again my wildest yells brought no reply, and I was going away to leeward again when I brought her up with the anchor. Then, lowering the sails, I rolled myself up in the mainsails to thaw my numbed body. After this brief respite from the buffeting of icy wind and spray, I hove up the anchor, hoisted sails, and beat up again to the ship; and this time the mate threw me a rope over the stern, and I made fast.

Then, after bending a rope round the unconscious bo'sun, and seeing him hoisted aboard, I climbed the rope myself, and as I touched the deck, dripping wet and dropping with fatigue, the mate said 'Get out of your wet duds, and turn to at once shifting ballast!' After that it was load wheat by day and the same nightly performance.

Sea Freezing Over.

So the days passed, with ever increasing coldness, till the old man sobered up sufficiently to realize that if he didn't get out of Berdianski soon he would not get away at all, for the Sea of Azov was fast freezing over. In a frenzy of haste, therefore, we finished loading in 14 days, working day and night, lying on our tummies to pack the wheat up tight to the beams with hand scoops. Then we set sail for Kertch, with the hope of some rest for our aching bodies.

This then is a slight sketch of life at sea in my boyhood days 60 years ago. But the 'Blair Athol's' end came before our time was out - and we boys were transferred to the 'Argosy' to finish our apprenticeship. And here befel an incident which might have finished it indeed!

In South America on the 'Argosy'

We took coals from Shields to Monte Video, and sailed from there in ballast to Valparaiso and Iquique for saltpetre. We were 28 days out, and 30 miles south of Valparaiso, and had just made the land when the wind fell away to a dead calm. There was a heavy swell rolling in shore, where three or four miles off, the stark, perpendicular mountain sides came down to a bottomless sea. There was no possible anchorage, and with the four or five other ships in our company we were being slowly rolled to our doom. The only thing between us and destruction was muscle. So we put out our boat, with the four men rowing, to pull the ship from the jaws of death. A frail tug surely to be pitted against the relentless force of the open Pacific swell. We toiled and strained through the long hours of that day and night, towing a ship with four men's arms against the might of the ocean swell, which, lifting the ship's jib-boom with every roll, carried the boat back and broke several oars. On Monday morning a puff of wind blew from the shore, and we came into the haven where we would be.

On our homeward voyage from Iquique we narrowly missed the worst of sea tragedies - no water! Before leaving Valparaiso we filled up from the water boat our 400 gallon tank,and the 2,000 gallon main tank, while the four 100 gallon casks on deck were kept filled from the water boat running up the coast. After about 30 days out our deck casks were empty, and the 400 gallon tank was down to a few inches of thick, rusty mud, so our old negro cook broached the main tank for tea. When we tasted the tea we all repaired to the galley to tell him what we thought of it. He shipped the pump again and made some more, with the same result. Our whole fresh water supply was salt! Investigation only deepened the mystery and consternation. The tank was perfectly sound, and filled with salt water. The old devil in the water boat, running short, had pumped it in from the sea.

We were straightaway put on rations of three half pints daily of rusty mud as black as ink, which lasted us a fortnight, battling all the time with N.E. gales. On the day of the last serving out, after mopping up the tank with rags, and squeezing out the last drop, we made the Falkland Isles.

Back in Deal.

At the end of this voyage I passed for second mate at the age of 19, and returned to Deal for Christmas with my certificate in my pocket. And there it was destined to remain for many weary months. I could not have struck a less favourable opportunity for putting it into action. All the January wool ships were coming in, nothing was sailing. Paid off ships' companies were already haunting the docks for the first ship outward bound. The docks were crowded with stately ships, but still more crowded with men waiting to sign on. Moreover, such was the fashion of those times that the very beauty of my clean-shaven young face went against me, when all men of sufficient maturity went bearded like the Pard.

'Do you want a second mate, sir?' I would boldly enquire of a likely looking skipper.

185

'Do I want a what?' he would roar in reply. 'Yes, I do want a second mate, but I want a man, not a beardless boy! Come back when you have some hair on your face!'

'The Cimba.'

It was many years before Holmes got his most famous command - 'The Cimba'. He describes her as follows:

'The iron ship 'Cimba' was built in 1878 by Walter Hood, of Aberdeen for the house of Nicol. She was painted green with the yellow stripe with white paint on deck and aloft. Her figurehead was the Scottish lion, from which she took her name. From her first till her last three voyages she was always a wool clipper, and over the whole of her 29 years under the British flag she averaged 89 days both ways between London and Australia - with 75 days as her record twice home, and 71 days on the outward trip.

She had only two British masters, Captain Fimister, who took her from the stock, and myself, who had her from 1895 till 1906. She was very heavy aloft and very narrow, and this made her extremely tender; but she was very, very pretty, and much loved by both her skippers, at any rate, and certainly by most of the men who sailed in her.

On my first outward trip we experienced little of note, till we passed the Cape, when we suddenly struck a gale with the heaviest sea I have ever seen in my life. It was a perfect, clear sunny day, with a bright blue sky, but at 4 a.m. when I came up on deck, it started howling like all the demons let loose. I shortened down the main top'sail, lower top'sails, and foresail; but she raced before the wind like a thing possessed. Mountainous seas were running after the ship, and she covered 336 miles that day, averaging 16 to 17 knots. But there was fiendish purpose and cruel tragedy in those diabolic curling waves, for one of them took my second mate, and no one knew the going of him.

In 1896 she did the trip home in 75 days, averaging eight knots for the voyage and this represents the best I ever got out of her. We left Sydney in company with the 'Argonaut' and 'Thessalis,' and twice on the voyage home I was in company with the 'Thessalis' who fairly romped away from the 'Cimba.' But she reported only one hour ahead of me, and the 'Argonaut' came up a month later.

One Day To Spare.

On her fifth voyage, the 'Cimba' missed Sydney, ranging as far as Rockhampton and Brisbane in her quest, so elusive was the Golden Fleece becoming for its early carriers, and we left Brisbane with a bare ninety-odd days to save the November wool sales. However, we got them, with one day to spare. But it was touch and go to the very last for we got stuck outside the Channel with easterly winds and hazy weather. I made in close to the Scilly Isles, and the day before our time was up I stood in to the Bishop's lighthouse to report, and seeing that everything depended on this I stood in till I could see the lighthouseman. But remembering the occasion when our signals were not reported, I stood off all night, and at 8 a.m. stood in to St. Mary's Signal Station till I saw the answering pennant. It was well I did so, or the sales would have been lost after all, and 1/16th d. a pound freight on wool made all the difference on the turnover of the voyage.

No longer a wool clipper.

On my eighth voyage, in 1903, the dainty little 'Cimba' for the first time left the track of the wool clippers, for on discharging at Brisbane, she went in ballast to load barley at Valparaiso. It was there, on June 3rd, that I put in the very worst night I have ever experienced at anchor.

From 8pm to 8am a northerly gale blew with increasing fury, and with 30 to 40 ships at anchor in that open bay, exposed to the full force of the Pacific, the night was rent with signals of distress, which could not be answered. No-one knew which would be the next cable to part, or who would survive the night; and morning revealed a piteous sight. The fine ship 'Foylesdale,' of Liverpool, was blown

187

ashore with great loss of life, two Chilean ships were dashed to pieces on that forbidding shore, while of the Pacific Mail S.S. 'Arequipa' not a trace remained. She had gone down with all hands. The 'Cimba' could not have held out much longer, she was dragging till she was under the bows of an Italian ship. On shore the toll of disaster was also high. Great stone blocks from the sea front were hurled far inland, while the railway lines were torn up and twisted round each other like giant corkscrews.

Personal Pride.

During all the years I was in command I was very fortunate in having good weather, and good crews; and it is a comforting reflection for a man who has spent 54 years of his life upon the world of waters to recall that he has never had a ship in trouble, nor even lost a suit of sails, though carrying them long after they might have been reefed down. But I always had good gear, and I had men and officers who could be depended upon. Many of them sailed with me voyage after voyage (one indeed for 20 years), and they each had a personal pride in the ship's achievement, and perhaps some faith in her skipper - for we had no grousers on board, even when driving through the vilest weather - and we always found time for diversions in fine weather. Wrestling and boxing contests were popular, and the boys were quite good at staging impersonations of Capt. Kettle, while music from fiddle, accordion, or mouth organ has a soothing, wistful quality on a lonely waste of water.

At Christmas time I was always called upon to assume the role of 'Santa Claus,' for the boys made a huge canvas stocking, which was pinned outside my cabin door with a delicate hint for its use, and a touching verse of greeting. Those boys were certainly young devils for getting round the Old Man - but they were good lads - all of them. I would never have unnecessary work done on Sundays or holidays, for men who work well deserve some rest, and life is hard enough at all times at sea. Nature sees to that, without human ingenuity adding anything to its hardship.

The 'Cimba's' Grave.

On her last voyage, the 'Cimba' loaded for Sydney, and it seems fitting that the little wool clipper, so well known in Sydney all her life, should make her farewell to Sydney when she was, all unwittingly, so near the end of her career. Destiny was surely foreshadowing her doom in sending her to Newcastle to load coals for Callao. It was the first time the dainty yacht-like ship had to suffer the indignity of carrying coals. It was also the last. Yet on this trip, all unconsciously, as her Swan Song, she made her last record for 'sail,' going from Callao to Iquique in 15 days.

She discharged her nitrate in Rotterdam. Then the blow fell. Mr. John Nicol, the practical man of the firm, died suddenly, and all the ships were sold. So passed one of the best firms of shipowners, and another beautiful ship went to the foreigners. The 'Cimba' herself found a grave in the Gulf of St. Lawrence some years later. And perhaps it was better fate than that reserved for so many beautiful ships, which, as freights become ever more elusive, were dismantled for coal hulks, and condemned to lie forgotten and forlorn, a very travesty of their former pride and beauty.

The ignominy of such an end is more cruel than their merciful oblivion of the waves.

In 1910, on the voyage home from Pt. Wakefield with wheat, we experienced some of the vilest weather I have ever known. On May 19th in long. 159 W., lat. 50 S. we ran into a hurricane which lasted till June 4th - undoubtedly the longest spell in inexpressibly beastly weather in my experience - for it was just one long unmitigated horror without a break or the sign of a break. For the whole time we were running for dear life under the lower top'sails only, with fifty times too much wind, snow and lightning day and night, pitch darkness alternating with hellish lightning which tore the heavens open with blinding flashes and left intensified blackness - such blackness that for 16 days we could not see a man on deck. And during the whole 16 days the devouring seas following us were curling up behind like mountainous canopies, and it was only the fact that she was stripped down that saved her from having her decks swept clean.

189

Everyone was wet through continually slithering about on the constantly falling snow, and, the galley fires being washed out, cut off even the comfort of hot coffee. But the worst feature of this decidedly unpleasant period was the number of corposants* which appeared aloft every night - eerie, creeping things, well called the 'Souls of dead sailors.' There is something uncanny in the sight of these phosphorescent-looking balls crawling out on the yard arms, down the backstays, up on the maintruck, as if impelled by some demoniac power. Never before have I seen so many of the accursed things, nor ever in these latitudes.

* A corposant is a ball of light sometimes seen about the masts or yard-arms of a ship during a storm. It is also known as St. Elmo's fire.

Boxing Day Sports.

We rounded the Horn on June 10th. On my last trip in the ship we were celebrating Boxing Day with sports, when we fell in with the Welsh ship 'Celtic Glen,' which passed quite close to us, in lat. 4S, long. 28W. Her men were shipping iron rust, and doubtless thought our crew were all mad and the Old Man drunk, seeing them skylarking about at sports.

The War.

Now for my new ship.* We left Newcastle, NSW, on June 2nd, 1914, with 2,356 tons of coal for San Francisco, expecting to arrive there at the beginning of August. Little did we dream that the World catastrophe was timed for the same date! Nor could we realize that we should thank our lucky stars for all our bad luck, when the wind fell away to dead calm and we could make no headway. On September 1st I sighted an American tanker, 'El Secundo,' I signalled her, asking my position, as I had not seen the sun for nine days.

190

He gave it, adding, 'Do you know your country is at war with Germany? And there are two German cruisers round here, been looking for you for the last month. You'd best get within the three-mile limit.'

It was good advice, but quite useless to a becalmed ship. However, the American backed it with practical assistance; for he wirelessed my position to San Francisco, and a tug came out to meet us. When I got in, I learnt from the papers that the 'Scharnhorst' and 'Leipzig' had been patrolling that coast since August 4th in need of coal, and I was the only British vessel due there with it. However, the delay which had fretted our souls had worn out the enemy's patience also, for they had left the vicinity that very week.

We left San Francisco on October 22nd with 2,300 tons of wheat and barley, and this time there was no difficulty in getting a cargo. The difficulty was in delivering it. The 'Invermay,' which left Portland Oregon just in front of us, was sunk between Falkland Isles and Monte Video by the Germans, who escaped from the Falkland Island battle, but of this of course, we knew nothing. The 'Invercoe' was likewise sunk about the same time, and the 'Inverlyon' got home from Portland Oregon with her wheat, and was just making Queenstown when a submarine sank her by gunfire. The ship's company escaped in two boats, one of which rowed 150 miles before landing.

* Strangely, Holmes does not tell us her name.

Knell Already Sounded

So my owners Messrs. Milne and Co. were pretty hard hit in a very short time, and whereas I left Newcastle in June 1914 as one of a paying fleet of sailing ships, when I reached home their knell had already sounded. Those that survived the Huns were quickly sold before further disaster befell them, for Milne's ran their ships uninsured, and no firm could long stand up to these losses.

I got my wheat to Queenstown and then to Grimsby without other incident than the sighting of dead man o'wars men near the Line and the narrow shave from a torpedo off the Isle of Wight, and then I offered my services to the Admiralty in any capacity, as did almost my entire ship's company. Months rolled on and nothing came of my application, and a further effort elicited the information that I was over age!

My Last Command

But I was not then so old as when I took up my next command in 1920. By that time the war was a thing of the past, and most of its heroes were struggling with the grim realities of peace. I had by that time given up all thought of further command, so few were the sailing ships left. But on March 31st I received a telegram from an old acquaintance, Captain Rugg who during the war had been trading between Bunbury, Mauritius and Singapore in the Bq. 'Dee' until she was sunk by the German raider 'Wolf' off Australia in 1916.

In 1920 Captain Rugg was taking out a schooner, 'The Gardner Williams,' to his owners in Mauritius to replace the 'Dee;' but he was so ill, through his two years internment in Germany, that he had to put back into Holyhead and wired me to take over his command. Thus it came to pass that my sea chest was packed again; the midnight express landed me in Holyhead on the morning of April 1st, and so I went down to the sea again.

My latest and last command looked ludicrous at first to a man who had spent all his life in square rigged ships, but I grew to like her well, when I had sailed in her, for she was a most comfortable and easily handled vessel. She needed to be, for her whole company consisted of 12 all told, four A.B.'s in each watch. Built of wood at Portland, Oregon, during the war, she was bought by the De Beers S. African Diamond Co., for £50,000 as the cheapest way of getting their machinery out to Africa! And then they sold her to the Mauritius timber merchants for £25,000. (The beautiful little 'Cimba,' with her teak wood, mahogany, and brass work, was sold for £3,500.)

After handing over the 'Gardner Williams' in Mauritius, I returned home round the old Cape route, for the first time in my life as a passenger. Yet 'ere I write 'finis' to the story, I would recall with pleasure those many shipmates of mine - skippers under whom I served with pleasure and respect, fellow skippers whom I met in many waters, and all the officers, boys and men who so loyally served me. I would also salute those of the great brotherhood who have sailed beyond this earthly horizon and made their last port.

Finally, I would pass on these memories to the sailors of to-day and to-morrow; the lads who plough the Seven Seas with coal, oil, and gas engines; but who never knew, and now never can know, the thrill of pitting skill and muscle against primeval forces - the pride in splendid achievement, the excitement of racing for months with unseen rivals, the fellowship born of spending months together with one common interest, the ship and the weather, the privations, starvation, misery and cold, which made up life at sea; and above all, the joy and pride in that loveliest work of man - the stately British sailing ship.'

Sailing Ships in the Downs by moonlight